EMBARRASSING MOMENTS
IN FRENCH

and how to avoid them

A Practical, Entertaining Guide
to Using French Correctly

SEYMOUR RESNICK
and
DORIANE KURZ

UNGAR / NEW YORK

1988

The Ungar Publishing Company
370 Lexington Avenue
New York, NY 10017

Sixth Printing 1988

Printed in the United States of America

Library of Congress Cataloging-in-Publication Data

Resnick, Seymour.
Embarassing moments in French and how to avoid them.
1. French language—Errors of usage.   2. French
language—Conversation and phrase books—English.
3. French language—Spoken French.   I. Kurz, Doriane.
II. Title.
PC2460.R4   1987   448.3' 421   87-5891
ISBN 0-8044-6706-4

ABOUT THIS BOOK

This little book had its origin in Paris. It was inspired by the remarks of numerous tourists about the inadequacy of their French. Most of them had studied the language at school for several years, but somehow they were unable to cope with the French of France. Our aim is to help supply the "missing link" between school French and the real thing. Each of the four sections fills a need not generally covered in the classroom.

Part I deals with deceptive homonyms (words that look or sound alike) and cognates (words of the same origin). They present serious pitfalls and may lead the English-speaking student of French into embarrassing blunders. Several examples will suffice: If you hear someone ask for a *blonde* at a café, don't turn around. He's only ordering a glass of beer. *Elle a bonne mine* means "she looks well," and has no reference to underground wealth. In a museum don't translate the caption *Nature Morte* as "Dead Nature"; it means "Still Life." And don't try to get a room at the *Hôtel de Ville*, because it's the City Hall.

There are literally thousands of these deceptive demons. We have attempted to include only those words which are of practical value. Here and throughout the book we have borne in mind the following criterion: Will the language-conscious tourist be likely to encounter this expression during a three-months' stay in France?

Part II presents important vocabulary and expressions not usually taught in school, but which *are* used in France.

Part III deals with essential slang and colloquial expressions. This important aspect of modern French is beyond the scope of most classrooms and dictionaries. Yet without a knowledge of the most popular of these expressions not only the spoken language, but a considerable portion of contemporary literature will be unintelligible. It is neither expected nor desired that the student proceed to use these slang and colloquial terms freely. On the contrary, they are presented primarily for recognition purposes, though their occasional use under proper circumstances will give one's French the Gallic flavor so few foreigners achieve. Further, a knowledge of some slang is indispensable to warn against possible embarrassing *faux pas*. There are a number of innocent words taught in school texts which are taboo because they have a vulgar connotation in current slang.

To keep this section as practical as possible and down to reasonable length, we have applied the "three-months test" mentioned above. We have also excluded unprintable vulgar expressions. The linguistically inclined tourist, however, will learn them soon enough if he travels in the right circles!

In this part as well as in the first two, almost all entries are used in illustrative sentences.

The final section attempts to help the tourist in some of the puzzling situations that will confront him in France. It may be read with profit even by those who do not know French. It is by no means a formal guide book dealing with places to see. But it does contain in concise form many useful items and practical tips often neglected in more elaborate travel books. Helpful hints will save the reader many francs and make his trip more pleasant. Situation vocabulary is supplied to help overcome linguistic difficulties.

In addition to its value to the tourist in France and to the prospective tourist at home, this book should serve a useful purpose in the schools. It would fit into an advanced course in practical French and may also be used to advantage as a supplementary text at almost any level.

CONTENTS

I. APPEARANCES ARE DECEIVING

How to avoid the pitfalls of words that look alike, but aren't

abuser. In addition to its English equivalent meaning, it often can be translated by "to take advantage of." *Elle abuse de ma patience:* she is taking advantage of my patience.

accuser. Besides having the general English meaning of "to accuse," it has a wide use in commercial correspondence in the expression *accuser réception de:* to acknowledge receipt of. Note also its interesting meaning in the expression *accuser son âge:* to show one's age.

achever. Be careful never to translate this by "to achieve." It merely means "to finish, to end." *As-tu achevé de lire ton livre?:* did you finish reading your book?

to achieve: *exécuter, accomplir.* I learned that he was able to achieve his plan: *j'ai appris qu'il a réussi à exécuter son projet.*

acquit. The noun *acquit* has very little in common with the English "acquittal" (*acquittement*). Its most specific use in French is commercial. It means "receipt." If on a bill you should find written *pour acquit,* that will mean "paid." But *faire quelque chose par manière d'acquit* or *par acquit de conscience:* to do something just to be able to say one has done it, i.e., carelessly, perfunctorily.

actif. Besides having the English meanings of "active, alert, brisk" it is used in business to mean "assets" (on a

9

balance sheet). *C'est une compagnie à actifs de $4.000.000:* this is a firm with $4,000,000 assets.

avoir à son actif: to have to one's credit

action. In addition to rendering the idea of the English word "action," it has a wide usage in the business world where it means "share, stock." *Les actions de la société* is not "the actions of society," but "the company's shares."

actuel. Means "present, of the present day, existing" and not "actual," which is rendered by *réel, véritable. Les conditions actuelles ne sont pas favorables à la prospérité:* existing conditions are not favorable to prosperity.

actuellement: at the present time

actualités: newsreel

addition. Besides being used in the English sense of "addition," this will be a very useful word in restaurants and cafés where you will ask for the bill by saying *l'addition, s'il vous plaît:* the bill, please. A "hotel bill," however, is *la note.*

affaire. The range of meanings of this word is much wider than that of its English cognate. In addition to meaning "affair" in the broad English sense, it also is the ordinary term used for "business." *C'est un bon homme d'affaires:* he is a good businessman. *Ils parlent affaires:* they are talking business. It may mean "things." *Mettez vos affaires sur la chaise:* put your things on the chair.

Mêlez-vous des vos affaires!: mind your own business!

connaître son affaire: to know one's business. *Je vais vous envoyer un électricien qui connaît son affaire:* I will send you an electrician who knows his business.

agent. Besides meaning "agent," this is commonly used in France for "policeman." The complete and correct expression would be *agent de police,* but you will find that Frenchmen will just tell you *l'agent vous donnera les renseignements que vous désirez:* the policeman will give you the information you desire.

agréer. Never means "to agree" in the sense of "to be of the same mind" (which would be rendered by *être d'accord*). It is best translated by "to accept, to approve." *J'ai agréé ses excuses:* I accepted his apologies. *J'ai agréé le contrat:* I have approved the agreement. In letters, *agréez mes salutations sincères:* yours sincerely.

agrément. Do not translate by "agreement." It means "pleasure, amusement, charm." *J'ai fait un voyage d'agrément en Italie:* I took a pleasure trip to Italy.

The idea of "agreement" is best rendered by *contrat* or *accord.* I entered into an agreement with him: *j'ai fait un contrat avec lui.* I am in agreement with you: *je suis d'accord avec vous.*

aimable. Not only "amiable" but also "kind, nice, good." *Vous êtes trop aimable, monsieur:* that is very kind of you.

air. Besides meaning "air," this word, depending on the context, may also be translated by "look, expression, appearance." *Vous avez l'air abattu aujourd'hui:* you have a downcast look today.

avoir l'air: to seem, look. *Votre ami a l'air très intelligent:* your friend looks very intelligent.

courant d'air: draft

Note that *air* may also mean "tune." *L'orchestre jouait*

un air très gai: the orchestra was playing a very merry tune.

amateur. Apart from the English meaning of "non-professional," it often means in French "lover, fan." *C'est un amateur des beaux-arts:* he is a lover of fine arts. *Mon beau-frère est un grand amateur de boxe:* my brother-in-law is a great boxing fan.

amende. Sometimes this does mean "amends" in the sense of "apology" (*faire amende honorable:* to make due apology), but usually it simply means "fine." *J'ai été forcé de payer l'amende pour excès de vitesse:* I was forced to pay the fine for speeding.

    sous peine d'amende: under penalty of fine

amuser. Like "to amuse" in English but note that the reflexive *s'amuser* means "to have a good time, to enjoy oneself." *Amusez-vous bien!:* have a good time!

ancien. This word not only means "ancient," but also "old, former." Actually, "ancient" is more often better rendered by *antique. J'ai organisé un dîner pour mes anciens copains d'école:* I have arranged a dinner for my former school chums.

annonce. Sometimes has meaning of "announcement," but is most frequently used in the sense of "advertisement." *J'ai inséré une annonce pour un emploi:* I placed an ad for a job.

    By extension, *annonces lumineuses:* neon lights.

    annonce de spectacle: playbill

anonyme. Like "anonymous," but in addition used commercially in the expression *société anonyme:* limited liability company, or incorporated. *Dumas, S.A.:* Dumas, Ltd. or Dumas, Inc.

anticipation. Besides its English meaning, it also means "advance" (of money). *Ils m'ont demandé de payer par anticipation:* they asked me to pay in advance.

appareil. Never translate by "apparel" (*habillement, vêtement*). It can mean "display, pomp" but is more commonly used for "device, apparatus, system."

appareil digestif: digestive system

You will also hear a camera most commonly referred to as *appareil. J'ai pris d'excellentes photos avec cet appareil:* I have taken excellent pictures with this camera.

On the telephone, *M. Durand à l'appareil:* Mr. Durand speaking.

appointements. Be careful not to be tempted to translate this by "appointment," which in French is rendered by *rendez-vous* or, if it is a business appointment, by *entrevue. Appointements* is always used in the plural and means "salary." *Il a touché ses appointements:* he has drawn his salary.

argument. Does not mean "dispute, quarrel" (*querelle, discussion*). It has the narrower meaning of "reason, proof." *Vos arguménts, monsieur, ne sont pas valables:* your arguments, sir, are not valid.

Argument is also the "main plot" or "summary" of a literary work.

armoire. Not "armory" (*arsenal, salle d'armes*) but "cupboard, wardrobe, closet." *Je vais mettre mes robes dans l'armoire:* I am going to put my dresses in the wardrobe.

arranger. As English "to arrange" but, in addition, "to suit, to mend, to tidy." *Arrange ta coiffure:* tidy (up) your hair-do. *Votre projet m'arrange très bien:* your plan suits me fine.

artifice. As English cognate, but *feu d'artifice:* fireworks.

assister. When *assister* is followed by *à*, do not translate by "to assist" but rather by "to be present at, to attend." *J'ai assisté à la partie de tennis:* I attended the tennis game.

When *assister* is not followed by *à*, then it may be translated by "to assist, to help." However, "to help" is more commonly translated by *aider*.

attendre. Not "to attend" but "to wait." *Je l'ai attendu plus d'une heure:* I waited for him over an hour. The idea of "to attend" may be rendered by *assister, être présent à*.

attention. As English cognate, but also commonly used as warning. *Attention!:* look out! *Attention! travaux en cours:* caution! repairs in progress.

avantageux. Besides "advantageous, profitable," it is also "becoming" (of dress or hair-do). *Cette coiffure est très avantageuse:* this is a very becoming hair-do.

    prix avantageux: reasonable price

    conditions avantageuses: profitable terms

bachelier. Not an unmarried man (*célibataire, vieux garçon*), but "bachelor" in the academic sense: one who has completed the *baccalauréat*, the degree granted on finishing the *lycée* (roughly equivalent to American high school plus one year of college). Note that the degree is not the equivalent of an American bachelor's degree.

bail. Be careful, as this word never means "bail" but "lease." So when your landlord insists upon *un bail à long terme* remember that he merely wants "a long lease."

bail: *caution, liberté sous caution*

blesser. This word never means "to bless" (*bénir*). Translate by "to wound, hurt, offend." *Essayez de ne pas blesser son amour-propre:* try not to wound his vanity. *Il a été blessé pendant la guerre:* he was wounded during the war.

blonde. In addition to "blonde," this means "light beer." *Donnez-moi un bock de blonde:* give me a glass of light beer.

bonneterie. You can't buy a bonnet in a *bonneterie.* You will be able to get hosiery, gloves, and some other female accoutrements. As for bonnets and other headgear, you will have to go to a *modiste* (milliner).

brassière. Not a woman's underwear garment (*soutien-gorge*) but a child's sweater with buttons and sleeves. Aboard ship a *brassière de sauvetage* is a "life-jacket." Do not confuse with *brasserie* which is a tavern-type restaurant, or a brewery.

brave. This word not only means "brave" but also "honest, good, worthy." *C'est un brave homme:* he is a worthy fellow.

bride. Not "bride" (*épouse*) but "bridle."

brut. Besides "brute" it means "raw, unmanufactured, rough, gross." *C'est un diamant brut:* it is a rough diamond.

poids brut: gross weight
sucre brut: unrefined sugar

bulletin. In addition to the English meaning of "bulletin," it also means "ticket, receipt, certificate, form." *Veuillez remplir le bulletin de bagages:* kindly fill out the luggage registration form. *Bulletin de consigne:* baggage-room receipt.

bureau. In addition to "bureau," it also means "office." *Voilà mon bureau personnel:* this is my private office.

    bureau de postes: post-office

    bureau de renseignements: information office

    bureau de tabac: tobacco shop

cabine. This word means not only "cabin" but also "booth." *Y a-t-il des cabines téléphoniques ici?:* are there any telephone booths here?

    cabine de bains: room at bath house

cabinet. Besides meaning "cabinet" it is one of the terms for "lavatory," and it also appears in the following expressions:

    cabinet de dentiste: dentist's office

    cabinet de toilette: dressing room

    cabinet de travail: study

    cabinet noir: dark room (photography)

cadet. Apart from meaning "cadet" it is also "younger, junior." *Il est mon cadet de huit ans:* he is my junior by eight years. *Je désire vous présenter mon frère cadet:* I wish to introduce my younger brother to you.

canapé. Not only the well-known refreshment but also "sofa, couch."

carton. In addition to its English cognate meaning, it is the word for "cardboard." *Ce papier n'est pas assez épais, il me faudra du carton:* this paper is not thick enough, I shall need cardboard.

    carton à chapeaux: hat-box

    carton d'écolier: school-bag

causer. Not only "to cause" but also "to chat, talk." *Venez me voir demain, nous causerons un peu:* come and see me tomorrow, we'll chat a bit.

    causer de la pluie et du beau temps: to talk about the weather (about things of no importance)

chagrin. In addition to the English meaning of "chagrin," it means "sorrow, grief." *J'ai du chagrin de vous voir si malade:* I am grieved to see you so ill.

chance. Besides "chance, hazard," it also means "good luck, good fortune." *Il a eu plus de chance que de talent:* he has had more luck than talent. *Je lui ai souhaité bonne chance:* I wished him good luck.

    courir la chance: to run the risk

change. Not "change" (*changement*), but "exchange." Commercial usages:

    lettre de change: bill of exchange

    bureau de change: foreign exchange office

    taux or *cours du change:* rate of exchange

    Note "change" (small): *monnaie.* Keep the change: *gardez la monnaie.*

charmé. In addition to "charmed," also "delighted." Used to acknowledge introductions, as *charmé de faire votre* *connaissance, madame:* I am delighted to make your acquaintance.

circulation. Besides its English equivalent meaning, it is the French word for "traffic." *Un arrêt de circulation m'a mis en retard:* a traffic tie-up made me late. *La circulation est très intense à la Place de l'Etoile:* traffic is very heavy at the Place de l'Etoile.

circulation interdite: no thoroughfare
circulation en sens unique: one-way traffic
accidents de la circulation: road accidents
défense de circuler sur l'herbe: keep off the grass

cité. Sometimes means "city," but it is also used to indicate a "housing development." *Cité universitaire:* the group of students' lodgings (in Paris).

client. In addition to "client," it also means "customer." *Depuis que ce magasin s'est modernisé, il a acquis beaucoup de nouveaux clients:* since this store was modernized, it has gained many new customers. *Cette modiste est capable de tout pour faire une cliente:* to win a new customer that milliner is capable of anything.

coco. Not "cocoa" (the drink) which is *cacao, chocolat. Coco* has several interesting and divergent uses. It may mean "cocaine," or any drug sold secretly. It is also a term of endearment, something more or less equivalent to "my pet." It may be used pejoratively to mean "fellow"; *un sale coco:* a bad egg.

coconut: *noix de coco*

collège. Never means "college" (*université*). Depending on the context, it is translated either by "grammar school" or "high school."

collier. "Collar" only when applied to animals. *J'ai acheté un nouveau collier pour mon chien:* I bought a new collar for my dog. In all other cases translate by "necklace." *Elle a un magnifique collier de diamants:* she owns a magnificent diamond necklace.

combinaison. May mean "combination" but is also the common word used for ladies' "slips." *Est-ce que ma combinaison dépasse?:* is my slip showing?

comédien. "Actor" in addition to "comedian." *Sarah Bernhardt a peut-être été la plus grande comédienne française:* Sarah Bernhardt was perhaps the greatest French actress.

Comédie means "drama, play" in addition to "comedy." *La Comédie Française,* in Paris, is the home of French classical drama.

commander. In addition to the English meaning of "to command," it is the regular term for "to order." *Je vais écrire à ma couturière pour lui commander des robes:* I am going to write to my dressmaker to order some dresses. *J'attends Jean pour commander le menu:* I am waiting for John before ordering.

une commande: an order. *Nous accusons réception de votre dernière commande:* we acknowledge receipt of your last order.

compétition. Do not translate by "competition" (*concurrence*). It means "rivalry." *Il y a eu beaucoup de compétition pour ce poste:* there was much rivalry for this post.

commission. Besides "commission" it also means "message, errand." *J'ai demandé à sa mère de lui faire la commission:* I asked her mother to give her the message. *J'ai beaucoup de commissions à faire cet après-midi:* I have many errands to run this afternoon.

complet. Not only "complete," but also "suit" (of clothes). *Je vais mettre mon complet bleu demain:* I am going to wear my blue suit tomorrow.

Note that a bus that is filled displays the sign *Complet* and will not take on additional passengers.

café complet: coffee with a bun (which may be either a *croissant* or a *brioche*)

thé complet: tea with little tea sandwiches or cookies

complexion. Do not translate by "complexion" (*teint*) but by "constitution, temperament." *C'est un homme de complexion solide:* he is a man of solid constitution.

composé. Besides meaning "composed," it also means "compound." *Les temps composés du verbe:* the compound tenses of the verb.

contrôleur. Not only "comptroller," but also "inspector." *Tous les voyageurs donneront leurs passeports au contrôleur:* all passengers are to give their passports to the inspector.

corps. Be careful not to translate by "corpse" as it means "body." *Il a un corps bien musclé:* he has a well-developed body.

corpse: *cadavre*

correspondance. In addition to "correspondence" it means "communication" (between places), "connection" (between trains). *Cet autobus fait correspondance avec un train:* this bus connects with a train.

billet de correspondance: transfer ticket

corsage. In addition to "corsage," it is a "bodice" or sometimes "blouse." *La jeune femme avec le joli corsage rose s'appelle Julie:* the name of the young lady in the pretty pink blouse is Julia. *Il faudra faire des réparations au corsage de cette robe:* we will have to alter the bodice of this dress.

course. Does not mean "course" but "running, race." *Aimez-vous aller aux courses?:* do you like to go to the races?

Note the expression *faire des courses:* to go on errands.

course: *cours.* This history course looks interesting to me: *ce cours d'histoire me paraît intéressant.*

crû. In addition to meaning "crude," this word also means "raw." *Remets cette viande au feu, elle est encore crue:* put this meat back on the fire, it is still raw.

Cru may also mean the locality in which vines are grown. *Les meilleurs crus de Bourgogne:* the best Burgundy vineyards.

vin du cru: local wine

Note the popular expression *une histoire de son cru:* a story of his own invention.

dame. While in English the word "dame" has a pejorative connotation, in French it is the equivalent of "lady." *La dame avec qui vous m'avez vu hier soir est ma fiancée:* the lady with whom you saw me last night is my fiancée.

déception. It meant "deception" only in ancient French. Today it should be translated by "disappointment." *Dans la vie il faut s'attendre à des déceptions aussi bien qu'à des moments de bonheur:* in life one must expect disappointments as well as moments of happiness.

deception: *tromperie, duperie, fraude*

défendre. Besides having its English cognate meaning, it also means "to forbid, prohibit, maintain (an opinion), protect." *Il est défendu de fumer:* smoking prohibited.

faire quelque chose à son corps défendant: to do something under coercion

On ne peut se défendre de l'aimer: one can't help loving her.

Likewise, the noun *défense* has the same meanings.

défense d'entrer: no admittance

défense d'afficher: post no bills

défense de fumer: no smoking

défense de cracher: no spitting

défense de circuler: no traffic

délicieux. Besides "delicious" it also means "charming, delightful." *Sa soeur est vraiment délicieuse:* his sister is really delightful.

demander. Not "to demand" but "to ask." *Je lui ai demandé de me rendre visite:* I asked him to come and visit me. *Demander* may be equally used in the sense of "to inquire." *Demandez-lui dans quelle direction il faut aller:* ask him in what direction we should go.

on demande: wanted (in newspaper ads).

to demand: *réclamer, exiger.* This plant demands a great deal of care: *cette plante exige beaucoup de soins.*

déposer. In addition to having the English meaning of "to deposit," this word is also used in the sense of "to bring, take, put down." *Cet autobus vous déposera à l'hôtel:* this bus will take you to the hotel. *Vous pouvez déposer le paquet sur la table:* you may put the package down on the table.

déranger. This word not only means "to derange," but also "to put out of order, upset (plans), disturb." *La guerre a dérangé tous nos projets:* the war has upset all our plans. *Pardonnez-moi si je vous dérange:* please excuse me if I am disturbing you.

se déranger: to put oneself out, bother. *Ne vous dérangez pas, je l'ai déjà ramassé:* don't bother, I have already picked it up.

désagrément. Never means "disagreement." Translate by "annoyance, unpleasantness." *Toute cette publicité lui a attiré beaucoup de désagréments:* all this publicity has brought him lots of unpleasantness.

disagreement: *différence, désaccord, querelle, mésentente.* We had a little disagreement yesterday, but are going to make up today: *hier nous avons eu une petite querelle, mais nous allons faire la paix aujourd'hui.*

deshonnête. Do not translate by "dishonest" but by "improper, unseemly." *Malheureusement elle était soûle et s'est conduite d'une façon deshonnête:* unfortunately she was drunk and behaved improperly.

dishonest: *malhonnête.* I cannot recommend this maid

to you because I found her dishonest: *je ne peux pas vous recommander cette bonne parce que je l'ai trouvée malhonnête.*

désolé. In addition to meaning "desolate," it is the common word for "sorry." *Je suis désolé d'avoir tâché votre robe:* I am sorry to have spotted your dress. *Elle était désolée de ne pas être à temps:* she was sorry not to have been on time.

détail. It has all the English senses of "detail" and, in addition, is the usual term for "retail." *Son mari est marchand de détail:* her husband is a retail dealer.

en gros et au détail: wholesale and retail

disque. Besides "disk" it also means "record." *Il a une très belle collection de disques de jazz:* he has a very beautiful collection of jazz records.

distraction. In addition to the English meaning of "distraction," it is also a common word for "recreation, diversion." *La lecture est ma distraction préférée:* reading is my favorite recreation.

distribution. Not only "distribution" but equally "delivery (of letters), cast, casting." *La distribution du courrier se fait deux fois par jour:* there is mail delivery twice a day. *La distribution de cette pièce est réellement excellente:* the cast in this play is really excellent.

distribution des prix: prize-giving (done in schools at the end of each scholastic year)

domicile. As "domicile" but, contrary to English where it is used mostly in legal matters, it also has the more general meaning of "residence, house, home."

service à domicile: collection and delivery at customer's house

emprunt à domicile (sign in circulating libraries) : loan of books which can be taken home

dot. Not "dot" but "dowry." *Cette jeune fille, avec ses millions de dot, sera un parti intéressant pour quelque jeune ambitieux:* this girl, with her millions for dowry, will be an interesting match for some ambitious young man.

Note the popular expression *c'est un coureur de dot:* he is a fortune hunter.

dot: *point.* You have the habit of forgetting the dots on your i's: *vous avez l'habitude d'oublier de mettre les points sur vos i.*

However, to arrive on the dot: *arriver à l'heure tapante.*

douter (de). Same meaning as the English "to doubt," but the reflexive *se douter de* means "to suspect, surmise." *Je me doutais bien que vous aviez ce projet:* I suspected you had this plan. *Il avait avalé une épingle sans s'en douter:* he had swallowed a pin without suspecting it.

dresser. This never means "to dress" but "to set up, erect, set (the table)." *Veux-tu être gentille et dresser la table pour moi?:* would you be kind enough to set the table for me? *Pendant que nous parlions, il dressait les oreilles:* while we were talking, he was pricking up his ears.

Note the additional use of *dresser* as "to train" (animals). *Tous mes chats sont très bien dressés:* all my cats are well trained.

se dresser: to stand, rise. *Je me suis dressée sur la pointe des pieds pour mieux voir:* I rose on tiptoes to see better.

to dress: *s'habiller, habiller.* I need only ten minutes to dress: *je n'ai besoin que de dix minutes pour m'habiller.*

éditeur. Translate this word by "publisher."
maison d'édition: publishing house
editor: *rédacteur*

éducation. In addition to its English cognate meaning, this word can be translated, according to context, by "breeding, upbringing, rearing (of animals)." *C'est une personne sans éducation:* he is an ill-bred person.

embarras. "Difficulty, fuss, encumbrance, hindrance" in addition to "embarrassment." *Ne faites pas tant d'embarras pour si peu:* don't make so much fuss over such a trifle.
avoir l'embarras du choix: to have too much to choose from

embrasser. Not only "to embrace" but also "to kiss." Indeed, *embrasser* is the usual word for "to kiss," since *baiser* is taboo because of its slang meaning.
Je vous embrasse de tout mon coeur: with much love (letter ending).
Note that *embrasser* may occasionally mean "to adopt, take up (a career)" or "to contain, include." *Il a décidé d'embrasser la médecine:* he has decided to take up medicine. *Cette encyclopédie embrasse une infinité de connaissances:* this encyclopedia contains a wealth of knowledge.

émission. Besides having the meaning of "emission," it also means "broadcasting." *J'écoute l'émission de musique tzigane tous les jeudis:* I listen to the gypsy music broadcast every Thursday.

poste d'émission or *station d'émission:* broadcasting station

enchanté. Not only means "enchanted" in the English sense, but is also the usual expression to acknowledge introductions. *Enchanté, madame, de faire votre connaissance,* or simply *enchanté:* pleased to meet you.

enfant. More often than "infant" it means "child (boy or girl), youngster." *Les enfants de douze à quinze ans aiment généralement les contes d'aventures:* youngsters between the ages of twelve and fifteen generally like adventure stories.

    enfant trouvé: foundling

    faire l'enfant: to behave childishly

ennui. In English "ennui" means only "boredom." In French it also means "vexation, nuisance, annoyance, troubles." *J'ai eu beaucoup d'ennuis avec cette affaire:* I had lots of trouble with this business.

    Likewise, *ennuyer* means not only "to bore" but also "to vex, bother."

entretenir. This is never "to entertain" but "to maintain, support, keep up" or "to converse (with), talk (to)." *J'entretiens une correspondance avec lui depuis dix ans:* I have kept up a correspondence with him for the past ten years. *Il ne gagne pas de quoi entretenir sa famille:* he does not earn enough to support his family. *Je vais vous entretenir de mes projets:* I am going to talk to you about my plans.

    to entertain: *amuser*

envie. Usually means "desire, wish, longing," rather than the English cognate "envy." *Elle m'a écrit qu'elle n'a* *aucune envie de faire un si long voyage:* she wrote to me that she has no desire to make such a long trip.

essence. This word not only means "essence" but also "gasoline." *Pendant la guerre il était difficile de trouver de l'essence:* it was difficult to find gasoline during the war.

étiquette. Not only means "etiquette" as used in the English language, but is also the word for "label, ticket." *Je vous conseille d'attacher une étiquette avec votre nom et adresse à chacune de vos valises:* I advise you to attach a label with your name and address to each of your suitcases.

etiquette gommée: gummed label

éventuel. Do not translate by "eventual" but by "possible, contingent, uncertain." In other words, the adjective would not apply, as in English to things sure to occur, but rather to things which may occur. Likewise the adverb *éventuellement,* which in French has the meaning of "possibly," and the noun *éventualité,* which should be translated by "possibility, contingency." *Nous faisons des économies pour un voyage éventuel en Europe:* we are saving for a possible trip to Europe. *C'est une éventualité qui ne me semble guère probable:* this is a possibility which does not seem at all probable to me. *Sortie éventuelle:* emergency exit.

eventual: *final, définitif*

eventually: *définitivement, finalement, à la fin.* I am afraid that eventually she will leave her job: *je crains qu'à la fin elle ne quitte sa place.*

évidemment. "Certainly, of course, obviously," as well as "evidently." *Savez-vous traduire du français en anglais?*

Mais évidemment!: can you translate from French into English? But, of course! *Ce n'est évidemment pas la première fois:* it is not the first time, you understand.

Likewise, *évident* not only means "evident" but also "obvious, plain." *C'est évident:* that is obvious. *Il est évident qu'elle ne vous aime pas:* it is obvious that she does not love you.

exhiber. Its use in French is not as wide as in English. It merely means "to present, produce." *Veuillez exhiber vos passeports à la frontière:* kindly show your passports at the border.

    to exhibit (in a general sense) : *montrer*

    to exhibit (pictures) : *exposer*

    to make an exhibition of oneself: *se rendre ridicule*

expérience. Besides "experience" it also means "experiment, test." *Les expériences de Pasteur sont très connues:* Pasteur's experiments are very well known.

    an experienced person: *une personne expérimentée*

exposer. "To exhibit" rather than "to expose." *Je vais commencer à exposer mes tableaux l'année prochaine:* I will start exhibiting my pictures next year.

Likewise, *exposition* means "exhibition." *Venez donc avec moi voir l'exposition des derniers tableaux de Dufy:* do come with me to see the exhibition of Dufy's latest pictures.

Note that *exposition* also may mean "exposure" (in photography).

fade. Not "faded" but "insipid, tasteless, flat (of taste)." *Cette omelette est très fade; essayez d'y ajouter du sel:* this omelet is tasteless; try adding some salt.

Likewise, *fadeur* means "tastelessness, insipidity," and in the figurative sense, "pointlessness." *Elle est accablée par la fadeur de sa vie actuelle:* the pointlessness of her present life is too much for her.

to fade: *se fâner.* What a pity that these roses have faded so quickly!: *quel dommage que ces roses se soient fânées si vite!*

faible. This word is more general in meaning than the English "feeble." Translate, depending on context, by "deficient, poor, weak, sorry, slender." *C'est un faible d'esprit:* he is feeble-minded. *Cet homme a un caractère très faible:* this man has a very weak character.

faillir. Sometimes means "to fail," as in the expression *faillir à son devoir:* to fail in one's duty. It also has, however, the meanings of "to very nearly do something" or "to go bankrupt." *Malheureusement ma dernière entreprise a failli:* unfortunately my last company went bankrupt. *Il a failli mourir lors de sa dernière attaque:* he nearly died at the time of his last attack.

faillite: bankruptcy

to fail: *échouer.* Yesterday I failed my examination: *hier j'ai échoué dans mon examen.*

failure: *insuccès.* He will never be able to forget the failure of his play: *il n'arrivera jamais à oublier l'insuccès de sa pièce.*

fantaisie. Like the English equivalent "fantasy," but, in addition, *fantaisie* may mean "not genuine, imitation."

sirop de mures fantaisie: imitation blackberry syrup (containing blackberry flavoring and not made from real blackberries)

fastidieux. Not "fastidious" but "dull, tedious." *Ne m'ennuie pas avec ces détails fastidieux:* don't bore me with these dull details. *Ces repas au restaurant commencent à devenir fastidieux:* these meals in the restaurant are beginning to pall.

fastidious: *difficile (à satisfaire), délicat.* Try to reserve a beautiful room because he is very fastidious: *essayez de réserver une belle chambre parce qu'il est très difficile à satisfaire.*

fat. Do not translate by "fat," as it means "silly, conceited, vain." *Je n'ai jamais connu de pire fat:* I have never known a more conceited fool.

fat: *gras, gros.* I am going to go on a diet because I am too fat: *je vais me mettre au régime parce que je suis trop grosse.*

to get fat: *prendre de l'embonpoint*

femelle. As English "female," but use only with reference to animals because, when applied to persons, it has a vulgar connotation. *Ce chat, est-ce un mâle ou une femelle?:* is this cat male or female?

female (when applied to persons): *féminin, des femmes.* Men claim that vanity is a female weakness: *les hommes prétendent que la vanité est une faiblesse féminine.*

figure. Besides having the meaning of its English equivalent "figure," it also means "face, air, appearance." *Il a une figure très gentille:* he has a very nice face. *Elle est très bien de figure:* she is good-looking.

Likewise, *figurer* in addition to "to figure" also means "to act, appear." *J'ai figuré Hamlet sur la scène:* I acted Hamlet on the stage.

However, the reflexive *se figurer* means neither "to figure" nor "to appear" but "to imagine." *Vous ne pouvez pas vous figurer le plaisir que votre cadeau m'a fait:* you cannot imagine what pleasure your present gave me. *Figurez-vous que . . . :* would you believe that . . .

to figure: *calculer.* After I figured the cost, I decided it would be too expensive for me: *après avoir calculé les frais, j'ai décidé que ce serait trop cher pour moi.*

figure (number): *chiffre*

figure (shape of body): *taille, tournure.* What a fine figure she has since she lost weight!: *quelle belle taille elle a depuis qu'elle s'est amincie!*

figure of speech: *façon de parler*

fine. In addition to being the feminine of the adjective *fin,* it is also used as a noun to mean "best quality brandy." *Donnez-moi une fine à l'eau:* give me brandy and water.

fixer. This word not only means "to fix," but also "to settle, stare at, attract, determine, establish." *Le prix du tabac est fixé par le gouvernement:* the price of tobacco is established by the government. *Je l'ai fixé jusqu'à ce qu'il s'est retourné:* I stared at him until he turned around. *Je suis fixé sur son compte:* I know all about him.

fixe: set. *Tous les prix ici sont fixes:* all the prices here are set.

prix fixe (in restaurants) : table d'hôte meal

formidable. Not "formidable" like its English cognate, but "wonderful, marvelous, tremendous." *C'est un film formidable, il faut que vous alliez le voir:* it is a wonderful film, you must go and see it.

formidable: *redoutable.* He is a formidable adversary: *c'est un adversaire redoutable.*

friction. In addition to meaning "friction," it is the usual word for "massage, rubdown." For example, the barber may ask you if you wish *une friction.*

Likewise, *frictionner* means "to rub, give a rubdown." After the bath, I give myself an alcohol rubdown: *après le bain je me frictionne avec de l'alcohol.*

garder. Besides having the general meaning of "to guard," *garder* has many other translations, the most common of which are "to keep, protect." *Gardez la monnaie:* keep the change. *Avec le rhume que vous avez, ce serait prudent de garder votre chambre un jour ou deux:* with your cold it would be wiser to stay in your room for a day or two. *C'était si drôle que je n'ai pu garder mon sérieux:* it was so funny that I was not able to keep a straight face. *Gardez votre droite:* keep to the right.

se garder de: to refrain from, to abstain. *Gardez-vous de le lui dire:* mind you do not tell it to him.

Dieu m'en garde!: God forbid!

The noun *gardien* sometimes means "guardian" but

more often should be rendered by "caretaker, doorkeeper, guard (in a museum)." *J'ai demandé au gardien du musée quelles étaient les heures de visite:* I asked the museum guard what the visiting hours were.

gardien de prison: warden

génial. Not "genial" but "having genius, clever." *Ça, c'est une idée géniale!:* that's a clever idea!

genial: *gai, joyeux.* His genial nature makes everyone like him: *sa nature gaie le rend sympathique à tout le monde.*

génie. In addition to having the same meaning as the English "genius," this word also means "engineering, the engineers." *Mon frère était dans le génie:* my brother was in the engineering corps.

gentil. Neither "gentle" nor "genteel" but "nice, pretty, amiable, kind." *Il a une très gentille femme:* he has a very nice wife. *Quel gentil bébé!:* what a pretty baby! *Il a été très gentil avec moi:* he was very kind to me. *Soyez gentil et prêtez-moi votre stylo:* be a good fellow and lend me your pen.

gentle: *doux, aimable, tranquille.* She is very gentle with her children: *elle est très douce avec ses enfants.*

genteel: *de bon ton, comme il faut, distingué.* This is an inexpensive, though genteel restaurant: *c'est un restaurant pas cher mais comme il faut.*

glace. Not "drinking glass" (*verre*) but "looking glass, mirror." *Regardez-vous dans la glace, vous êtes tout ébouriffé:* look at yourself in the mirror, your hair is all mussed up.

Glace is also the common word for "ice" or "ice cream." *Je prendrai une glace au chocolat:* I'll take some chocolate ice cream. *Le morceau de glace que j'avais mis dans mon café a déjà fondu:* the piece of ice I had put into my coffee has already melted.

gracieux. This word may mean "gracious" but is generally better translated by "graceful." *Elle a de très gracieux mouvements:* she has very graceful movements.

Note that when *gracieux* does mean "gracious," it is followed by the prepositions *pour* or *envers. Elle s'est conduite d'une façon très gracieuse envers moi:* she behaved very graciously toward me.

grappe. This word does not mean "grape" (*raisin*) but "bunch (of grapes or currants)." *Une grappe de raisins:* a bunch of grapes.

    raisin: *raisin sec*
    grapefruit: *pamplemousse*

grief. Be careful not to translate this word by its English equivalent "grief." It means "grievance, wrong, injury." *Je ne lui pardonnerai jamais le grief qu'elle m'a fait:* I will never forgive her for the wrong she did me.

    grief: *chagrin, douleur.* Her grief at her sister's death was overwhelming: *sa douleur, lors de la mort de sa soeur, fut immense.*

habit. Do not translate by "habit" (*habitude*) but by "garment, clothes, suit, coat." *Il a tellement grandi qu'il faudra lui acheter de nouveaux habits:* he has grown so much that we will have to buy him new clothes.

35

être en habit: to be in evening dress

prendre l'habit: to enter the priesthood

halle. Not "hall" (*vestibule,* or English word "hall" may be used) but "market, market place." Usually, *une halle* or *les halles* is a covered market while *un marché* is an outdoor market. *Les halles à Paris s'ouvrent très tôt le matin:* the market places in Paris open very early in the morning. *Ma mère est allée à la halle mais elle sera bientôt de retour:* my mother went to market but she will soon be back.

hardi. Be careful not to translate this word by "hardy." It means "bold, fearless" or sometimes "insolent." *Le pianiste avait le jeu hardi:* the pianist had a bold touch. *Si ses manières n'étaient pas si hardies, il me serait très sympathique:* I would find him quite nice, if it were not for his forward manners.

hardy: *fort, robuste.* In spite of his delicate appearance, he is rather hardy: *en dépit de son apparence délicate, il est plutôt robuste.*

hasard. Besides having the meaning of "hazard," the word *hasard* may be more widely translated by "chance, probability, possibility, risk." *Je ne veux pas courir le hasard de la rencontrer:* I don't want to run the risk of meeting her.

par hasard: by chance. *Je l'ai su par hasard:* I learned about it by chance.

à tout hasard: at all events

au hasard: at random

hâte. Not "hate" (*haine*) but "hurry, speed, promptness."

Je vais lui téléphoner de venir en toute hâte: I will call him and tell him to come with all possible speed.

avoir hâte: to be in a hurry, to be anxious (to). *J'ai hâte de vous revoir:* I am anxious to see you again.

à la hâte: in a hurry

herbe. "Grass" as well as "herb." *Je vais me coucher sur l'herbe, à l'ombre du sapin:* I am going to lie on the grass, in the shade of the pine tree.

fines herbes: seasoning herbs

mauvaise herbe: weed; scamp (fig.)

hisser. Do not translate by "to hiss" but by "to hoist." *Les jours de fête nationale, on hisse les drapeaux:* the flags are hoisted on national holidays.

se hisser: to raise, to lift oneself up. *Hissez-vous sur la pointe des pieds, vous verrez mieux:* raise yourself on your toes, you will see better.

to hiss: *siffler.* In France, when a play is not liked, it is hissed by the public: *en France, lorsqu'une pièce ne plaît point, elle est sifflée par le public.*

histoire. In addition to meaning "history" in the English sense, it is also the word for "story, tale, anecdote." *Je vais vous raconter une histoire qui vous fera tordre de rire:* I am going to tell you a story which will make you split with laughter.

Some colloquial uses:

le plus beau de l'histoire c'était: the best of it was. *Le plus beau de l'histoire c'était qu'il a dû passer la nuit en prison:* the best of it was that he had to spend the night in prison.

histoire de: in order to. *Histoire de passer le temps, regardez cet album:* in order to pass the time, look at this album. *Histoire de rire:* just for fun; for the fun of it.

hommage. This word not only means "homage" as its English cognate, but also "respect, token." *Ses élèves lui ont donné en hommage une montre en or:* his students gave him a gold watch as token of gratitude. *J'aimerais rendre mes hommages à madame votre mère:* I would like to pay my respects to your mother.

avec mes hommages: with my compliments

honnête. Broader in meaning than the English equivalent "honest," this may also be translated by "decent, modest, reasonable, honorable, polite."

hôtel. Has a wider usage than the English "hotel." May mean "town house, hall" in addition to "hotel." *Il a un grand hôtel à Paris* could mean: he has a big hotel in Paris, or he has a large house in Paris.

hôtel de ville: town hall or city hall

hôtel des postes: General Post Office

l'hôtel-Dieu: chief hospital in many French towns

humeur. Generally translate by "mood, disposition, temper." *Je suis en humeur de faire une longue balade:* I am in a mood to take a long walk. *Tant qu'elle aura de l'humeur, elle ne vous adressera pas la parole:* as long as she is out of temper she will not speak to you.

Note also the Anglicism *humour:* sense of humor.

idiotisme. Not "idiocy" (*idiotie*) but "idiom, idiomatic expression." *Voulez-vous me faire une liste de tous les* *idiotismes dont vous vous souvenez en anglais?*: would you kindly draw up for me a list of all idiomatic expressions you remember in English?

Note that *idiot* is more commonly used in French than in English in the sense of "stupid, foolish." *Ne trouvez-vous pas que le film était vraiment idiot?*: don't you think that the film was really stupid?

ignorer. An easy and dangerous trap. In French *ignorer* means "not to know, to be unaware of," while in English "to ignore" means "to wilfully disregard." *Savez-vous que Robert est malade? —Non, je l'ignorais:* do you know that Robert is ill? No, I didn't know it. *Je n'ignore pas que ce soit difficile:* I know that it is difficult.

to ignore: *prétendre ignorer, ne tenir aucun compte de, ne pas vouloir reconnaître.* I don't care if he ignores me: *ça m'est égal qu'il ne veuille pas me reconnaître.*

impasse. In addition to the English meaning, the French word has also the literal sense of "blind alley, dead end." *Il faudra revenir en arrière car nous voilà arrivés à une impasse:* we shall have to turn back because we have come to a blind alley.

imperméable. Like its English cognate, but it is also the common word for "raincoat." *Je vous conseille de prendre votre imperméable et vos galoches car je suis sûre qu'il va pleuvoir:* I advise you to take your raincoat and your galoshes because I am sure that it is going to rain.

incessamment. Do not translate by "incessantly" but by "at once, immediately." *Je voudrais que vous le fassiez incessamment:* I would like you to do it at once.

incessantly: *sans cesse, sans relâche, continuellement.* He worked at it incessantly for two days: *il y travailla sans relâche pendant deux jours.*

inconvénient. Almost always better translated by "disadvantage, objection," although occasionally the context will allow you to render it by "inconvenience." *Je ne vois pas d'inconvénient à votre projet:* I have no objection to your plan. *L'inconvénient de l'affaire c'est que vous avez très peu de temps:* the disadvantage of the matter is that you have very little time.

inconvenience: *ennui, dérangement, difficulté.* The results will make you forget all the inconveniences: *les résultats vous feront oublier tous les ennuis.*

indication. This word is usually used in the plural to mean "particulars, details" rather than "indications." *Il m'a donné des indications détaillées sur cette voiture:* he gave me detailed particulars on this car.

indicateur: railroad timetable

inférieur. In addition to the English meaning of "inferior," it has also the physical sense of lower. *Seine-Inférieure:* Department of the Lower Seine. *Animaux inférieurs:* lower animals. *Lèvre inférieure:* lower lip.

infiniment. Generally has the same meaning as the English "infinitely." However, in expressions of obligation or thanks, the meaning of *infiniment* is weaker and should be rendered by "very much, extremely." *Je vous suis infiniment reconnaissant:* I am extremely grateful to you. *Merci infiniment:* thank you very much.

ingénuité. Do not translate by "ingenuity." It means "simplicity, lack of sophistication, artlessness." *Son ingénuité la rend très sympathique:* her lack of sophistication makes her very likeable.

ingenuity: *ingéniosité.* With his ingenuity, he would know how to get along even on a desert island: *avec son ingéniosité, il saurait se tirer d'affaire même sur une île déserte.*

injure. Means not only "injury" but also "insult, abuse." *Il m'a criblé d'injures:* he hurled insults at me.

"Injury" (in the physical sense) is rendered in French by *blessure, lésion.*

inscrire. Like English "to inscribe" but also "to enter (bookkeeping), register." *Je désire m'inscrire à l'université:* I wish to register for college. *Ayez la bonté d'inscrire toutes vos dépenses dans ce cahier:* kindly enter all your expenses in this notebook.

intoxication. If the doctor tells you you are suffering from *intoxication* do not think he is accusing you of drunkenness. He merely means that you have a touch of food poisoning!

intoxicant. Beware of a bottle thus labeled! It means "poisonous."

intoxication: *ivresse, enivrement*

introduire. Means "to introduce" only in the sense of introducing a topic into a conversation. Otherwise it has the physical sense of "to put in, stick in." *Je n'arrive pas à introduire la clé dans la serrure:* I cannot manage to put the key in the keyhole.

to introduce: *présenter*. Allow me to introduce my wife: *permettez-moi de vous présenter ma femme.*

invalide. Does mean "an invalid" as in English but note that *Les Invalides* is not a hospital as one might surmise from the name. It is one of the famous monuments and tourist attractions of Paris.

joindre. As English "to join" but has the additional meanings of "to combine, unite, enclose, clasp." *Vous trouverez ci-joint le texte anglais du contrat:* you will find herewith enclosed the English text of the contract. *Les enfants avaient joint les mains et étaient en train de tourner en rond:* the children had clasped hands and were going around in a circle.

journal. Remember that this is the regular word for "newspaper." It may also mean "diary."

juste. In addition to "just," it may also mean "right, exact, fitting, fair, tight." *Est-ce que votre montre est juste?:* is your watch right? *Mes bottes sont trop justes:* my boots are too tight.

    juste ciel, juste Dieu: good heavens, good Lord

    au juste: exactly, precisely. *Peux-tu m'expliquer au juste comment cela fonctionne?:* can you explain to me exactly how that works?

    tout juste: just, barely. *Nous arriverons tout juste à temps:* we will arrive just in time.

    six heures justes: six o' clock sharp

    chanter juste: to sing in tune

    le mot juste: the precise word

lard. Not "lard" (*saindoux*) but "bacon." *Donnez-moi une omelette au lard:* give me a bacon omelet.

lame. This is a noun in French for "blade" (for razors) and should not be confused with the English adjective "lame" (*boîteux*).

langage. Translate by "tone, style of speech, talk, words," rather than by "language." *Je vous prie de changer de langage quand vous vous adressez à vos supérieurs:* kindly change your tone when you speak to your superiors. *Elle dit que tous ses soupirants tiennent le même langage:* she says that all her wooers say the same thing.

Note that sometimes *langage* is used in the pejorative sense. *Il a un drôle de langage!:* that's a queer way of talking he has!

language: *langue.* They say that the English language is difficult to learn: *on dit que la langue anglaise est difficile à apprendre.*

bad language: *grossièretés.* Don't use such bad language: *ne dites pas de telles grossièretés.*

large. It is only very seldom that the context will allow you to translate this word by "large"; it generally means "broad, wide, generous." *C'est un homme d'idées larges:* he is a broad-minded man. *Je crois que la table que vous venez d'acheter sera trop large:* I think that the table which you have just bought will be too wide. *La chambre a 15 pieds de large:* the room is 15 feet wide.

au long et au large: in length and width

large: *grand, gros.* It seems to me that this overcoat is

too large for you: *il me semble que ce manteau est trop grand pour vous.*

lecture. This word is often and easily mistranslated; it does not mean "lecture" but "reading."

cabinet de lecture: reading room

lecture: *cours, conférence.* The history teacher gave a very interesting lecture on Napoleon: *le professeur d'histoire a fait une conférence très intéressante sur Napoléon.*

librairie. This word is another common pitfall in translations. It does not mean "library" but "bookshop, publishing house" or sometimes "circulating library."

library: *bibliothèque.* My thesis took several weeks of research at the library: *ma thèse a pris plusieurs semaines de recherches à la bibliothèque.*

license. Like English "license" but also means "university degree." *Il a sa license en droit:* he has a law degree.

marriage license: *dispense de bans*

location. Never translate by "location" (*situation, emplacement*). It means "letting out, renting, rental price, booking (of seats at theater), price of seats." *Le prix de la location de votre maison est trop élevé pour moi:* the rental price for your house is too high for me.

bureau de location: box office

lunatique. The French word is weaker in meaning than the English cognate. Render by "whimsical, fantastic, moonstruck." *Il est légèrement lunatique, mais il est très gentil:* he is somewhat odd, but very nice.

lunatic (mad): *fou.* A dangerous lunatic has escaped: *un fou dangereux s'est échappé.*

44

luxure. Be careful not to translate by "luxury" or rather not to use *luxure* when you want to convey the idea of "luxury." The French word means "lewdness, lust."

luxury: *luxe*. She has always liked luxury: *elle a toujours aimé le luxe*.

machin. Not "machine" which is spelled in exactly the same way in French as in English, but a word popularly used as a convenient substitute for almost anything whose name has been forgotten or is not known. *Donne-moi le machin pour déboucher la bouteille*: give me the contraption to unscrew the bottle. *Et machin, l'as-tu vu?*: and did you see what's-his-name?

magasin. Never means "magazine" in the sense of weekly or monthly publication (*revue, magazine*). Translate by "shop, store, warehouse." *Ma femme est en train de courir les magasins mais elle ne tardera pas à rentrer*: my wife is out shopping but she will soon be back. *Nous n'avons plus ce modèle en magasin*: we no longer have this model in stock.

maître. In addition to English "master," it is also the title given in France to lawyers. *Le requérant sera représenté par Maître Durand*: the plaintiff will be represented by Mr. Durand (his lawyer).

Note that in France only teachers of public schools (up to the *lycée*) are called *maître*. In secondary and higher education (*lycées* and universities) the teachers are called *professeurs*.

marche. Besides "march," it may mean "walk, conduct, step, stair, progress." *Venez, nous allons faire une petite marche:* come, we will take a little walk. *J'ai glissé sur la marche de l'escalier:* I slipped on the staircase.

   mettre en marche: to set going. *Ce ne sera pas facile de mettre en marche cette affaire:* it will not be easy to set this business going.

marcher. In addition to having the English meaning of "to march," it also means "to walk, work, run." *Cette montre marche très bien:* this watch works very well. *C'est sa femme qui fait marcher l'affaire:* it is his wife who runs the business. *L'ascenseur ne marche pas:* the elevator is not running.

   Note that in colloquial use, *marcher* means "to accept, do," and *faire marcher* means "to deceive, fool."

   Je marche: agreed. *Je ne marche pas:* no, sir, not me. *On m'a fait marcher cette fois-ci, mais on ne m'y reprendra plus:* they fooled me this time, but they won't catch me again.

marine. Equivalent to English "navy." Also note *marin:* sailor.

   bleu marine: navy blue

marque. In addition to "mark," it has in French the meanings of "brand, make, sign." *Je n'aime pas cette marque de rouge à lèvres:* I don't like this brand of lipstick. *Ces nuages ne sont pas forcément une marque de pluie pour demain:* these clouds are not necessarily a sign of rain for tomorrow.

   liqueurs de marque: liqueurs of superior quality

Note however that a "mark" in school should be translated by *note, point*. I received a very bad mark on my last examination: *j'ai reçu une très mauvaise note à mon dernier examen*.

mat. Never means "mat" in the sense of doormat, etc. When used as a noun it means "dullness" (of color, generally) or "mate" (in chess). When used as an adjective, translate by "dull, unpolished, lusterless." *Je suis échec et mat:* I checkmate. *Je trouve les coloris de ce tableau trop mats:* I find the colors of this painting too dull.

mat (straw door mat): *paillasson*
mat (placemat): *dessous de plat*

mémoire. When it is feminine it is equivalent to the English "memory" and may also be translated by "recollection, commemoration, remembrance." When it is masculine, translate by "bill, memorandum, treatise (literary)." *Je compte préparer un mémoire sur les moeurs des indigènes:* I intend to prepare a treatise on the customs of the natives. *Je vous enverrai un mémoire acquitté:* I will send you a receipted bill.

migraine. "Headache" not necessarily as severe as conveyed by the English term. *Je préfère ne pas sortir ce soir car j'ai la migraine:* I prefer not to go out tonight because I have a headache.

mine. It may mean "mine" as in English but it is also used in some very common expressions.

avoir bonne mine: to look well
avoir mauvaise mine: not to look well

faire bonne mine à quelqu'un: to greet someone pleasantly

faire la mine à quelqu'un: to pout at someone

faire mine de: to pretend to

faire mine de vouloir: to make as if to

avoir la mine trompeuse: to have a deceitful look

misère. Sometimes the context will allow you to translate this word by "misery" but it also means "distress, wretchedness, poverty, trifle." *Elle est morte de faim et de misère:* she died of starvation and want. *Ne vous irritez pas pour de telles misères!:* do not excite yourself for such trifles!

faire des misères à quelqu'un (colloq.): to afflict someone, grieve. cause worry. *Il nous a fait beaucoup de misères mais nous lui avons pardonné:* he has caused us a lot of worry but we have forgiven him.

Note that *misérable* means "wretch, destitute, miserable person" and also "villain."

monnaie. Not "money" (*argent*) but "change, small cash." *Je n'ai pas de monnaie pour le pourboire:* I have no change for the tip. *Si ça vous est égal, je vous paierai en monnaie:* if it is all the same to you, I will pay you in small change.

mortel. In addition to having the meaning of its English cognate, it may also be translated by "long, tedious, deadly, fatal." *Malheureusement sa maladie est mortelle:* unfortunately his is a fatal disease. *J'ai passé deux heures mortelles à bavarder avec ma voisine:* I spent two long hours talking to my neighbor.

nature. Not only means "nature," but also "life, life-size."
Il dessine d'après nature: he draws from life.

nature morte: still life

payer en nature: to pay in kind

omelette nature: plain omelet

café nature: black coffee

enfant naturel: illegitimate child

net. The French word has, in addition to the English sense
(net weight: *poids net*), a variety of meanings like "clean,
clear (of arguments), frank, pointblank." *Sa maison est
très nette:* his house is very clean. *Il m'a parlé d'une
façon très nette:* he spoke to me very frankly.

voir net: to see clearly, be clearheaded

refuser net: to refuse outright, give a flat refusal. *Je lui
ai demandé de me prêter de l'argent mais il m'a refusé net:*
I asked him to lend me money but he gave me a flat no.

avoir les mains nettes (colloq.): to have one's hands
clean; to have nothing to do with something

nombre. More restricted in meaning than its English equivalent. It means "number" only in the abstract sense. A
printed or written number (figure) is better rendered by
chiffre, while a telephone number or street number or number (issue) of a publication would be translated by
numéro. Ils sont venus en grand nombre à ses funérailles:
they came in great numbers to his funeral. *Il me semble
que, dans cette division, deux des chiffres sont inexacts:*
it seems to me that two of the figures in this division are
incorrect. *Voulez-vous avoir la gentillesse de me donner son*

numéro de téléphone? : would you be kind enough to give me his telephone number?

nomination. In French it usually means "election" or "appointment."

note. Not only "note" as in English but also "bill" (in a hotel) and "school mark, grade." *Si vous continuez à avoir de si mauvaises notes, vous ne passerez pas ce cours:* if you continue having such poor marks, you will not pass this course.

Note that a restaurant bill is *addition* and a commercial bill is *facture.*

notice. Translate by "notice" only when context indicates that it means notice in the sense of "review, critical comment." Otherwise, render by "sketch, account." *Le livre contient une notice biographique de l'auteur:* the book contains a biographical sketch of the author.

to notice: *remarquer, prendre connaissance de*

notice (announcement) : *avis.* Notice to the reader: *avis au lecteur.*

to give notice (company to employee) : *donner congé*

to give notice (employee to company) : *donner avis*

nouvelle. Never means "novel," but "novelette, short story." Also the common word for "news." *Avez-vous de ses nouvelles?* : have you any news of him? *Point de nouvelles, bonnes nouvelles* (proverb) : no news is good news. *Quelles nouvelles?* : what's new? *Vous m'en direz des nouvelles:* you will be delighted with it (lit., you will give me news of it).

novel: *roman*

obligation. Has all the general meanings of its English equivalent but, in addition, may mean in commercial terminology "debenture, bond."

Porteur d'obligation: bondholder

obscur. The regular word for "dark" as well as "obscure." *Il fait obscur:* it is dark. *Cette forêt obscure m'effraie un peu:* this dark forest frightens me a little.

dark (color): *foncé.* I look better in dark than light green: *le vert foncé me va mieux que le clair.*

occasion. Means "opportunity, chance, secondhand, bargain" more often than "occasion." *Profitez de cette occasion, vous ne le regretterez pas:* take advantage of this opportunity, you won't be sorry. *Sa maison est remplie de meubles d'occasion:* her house is filled with secondhand furniture. *A ce prix, c'est une occasion:* at this price, it is a bargain. *Vente d'occasions:* sale, bargains.

à l'occasion: in case of need, if need be. *A l'occasion, je pourrai vous prêter un peu d'argent:* if need be, I shall be able to lend you a little money.

occupé. In addition to "occupied" it also means "taken, busy." *Je serai très occupée cette semaine:* I will be very busy this week. *Est-ce que cette place est occupée?:* is this seat taken? *La ligne est occupée:* the line is busy.

office. This is occasionally used in the sense of the English word "office" as in *office de publicité* (advertising office). However, "office" is usually better rendered by *bureau. Office* is both feminine and masculine. The latter should be translated by "functions, service, turn," and the former by "pantry, servants' rooms." *C'est un office d'ami que vous* *me rendez:* you are doing me a friendly turn. *Demandez à la bonne d'aller chercher de la confiture à l'office:* ask the maid to bring some jam from the pantry.

ombrelle. Not "umbrella" *(parapluie)* but "parasol" *Promenez-vous avec une ombrelle quand il fait chaud:* use a parasol when it is hot.

opportunité. Does not mean "opportunity" but "opportuneness, seasonableness, expediency." *Il a immédiatement compris l'opportunité de cette mesure:* he immediately understood the opportuneness of this measure.

opportunity: *occasion.* Opportunity makes the thief: *l'occasion fait le larron* (proverb).

orateur. Besides meaning "orator," it is also the ordinary term for "speaker, spokesman." *L'orateur reprit son discours:* the speaker resumed his address.

ordonnance. Not only "ordinance," but also "order, regulation, arrangement, prescription (med.), orderly (army)." *Le pharmacien est en train d'exécuter l'ordonnance:* the druggist is filling the prescription.

orthographe. "Orthography" is a rather learned word in English but *orthographe* is the regular word in French for "spelling." *Vous faites très peu de fautes d'orthographe en français:* you make very few spelling mistakes in French.

parent. May mean "relative" in addition to "parent." *Je vais aller habiter chez des parents que j'ai à Paris:* I am going to live with some relatives I have in Paris.

parti. Not "party" in the sense of "social gathering" (*fête*). Besides meaning "part, party (organized group of people)" it may also mean "decision, match (marriage), advantage." *C'est le chef du parti socialiste:* he is the leader of the socialist party. *Quand mes deux frères se disputaient, je prenais toujours le parti du cadet:* when my two brothers argued, I always took the part of the younger one. *Cette jeune fille est un parti excellent:* this girl is an excellent match. *J'ai pris le parti de me taire:* I chose to be silent. *Elle cherche à tirer parti de tout:* she tries to turn everything to her own advantage.

un parti pris: a foregone conclusion

en prendre son parti: to resign oneself to the inevitable, to make the best of it

particulier. When used as a noun, it does not mean "particular" in the sense of "exacting" (*exigeant*) but "private, individual." *Ne me demandez pas l'impossible, je ne suis qu'un simple particulier:* don't ask the impossible of me, I am only a simple private person.

When used as an adjective, it has all the meanings of its English cognate, and in addition, those of "peculiar, private, special, odd." *Cette situation est fort particulière:* this is a very odd situation. *Je voudrais qu'on me donne une chambre particulière:* I would like them to give me a private room.

en particulier: especially. *J'ai beaucoup aimé votre livre, en particulier le dernier chapitre:* I liked your book very much, especially the last chapter.

particulars: *détails, renseignements.* Write to the Chamber of Commerce for further particulars: *écrivez à la Chambre de Commerce pour de plus amples détails.*

partie. In addition to "part" or sometimes "party" (in legal terminology), it may also mean "game, entry (bookkeeping)." *Voulez-vous faire une partie de tennis?:* would you like to play a game of tennis? *Ayez la bonté de vérifier ces parties doubles:* kindly check these double entries.

Voulez-vous être de la partie?: will you be one of us?

passionné. Not only "passionate" but also "enthusiast, fan." *Ma soeur est une passionnée du cinéma:* my sister is a movie enthusiast.

Likewise, *passionner,* in addition to meaning "to excite with passion," can also be translated by "to interest deeply." *Je suis convaincue que ce roman vous passionnera:* I am convinced that this novel will interest you deeply.

patron. Besides being used in the sense of its English equivalent, this word also may mean "boss" and "pattern." *Mon patron refuse de me donner une augmentation:* my boss refuses to give me a raise. *Quand commencerez-vous à découper le patron?:* when will you start cutting the pattern?

peine. Sometimes, though not often, "physical pain" (which is generally better rendered by *mal, douleur*); usually translate by "trouble, penalty, punishment." *J'ai eu beaucoup de peine à le convaincre:* I had lots of trouble in convincing him. *Certains pays ont aboli la peine capitale:* certain countries have abolished capital punishment.

se donner de la peine pour: to take pains to. *Elle s'est*

donné beaucoup de peine pour achever son travail à temps:
she took great pains to finish her work on time

donnez-vous la peine d'entrer: pray do come in

à peine: scarcely, hardly. *Il sait à peine lire:* he can
hardly read.

pension. Not only "pension," but also "boarding school,
boarding house, board and lodging." *Elle a mis ses enfants
en pension:* she placed her children at a boarding school.
Le prix comprend pension et chambre: the price includes
room and board.

pension de famille: residential hotel or boarding house

phrase. Not only "phrase" but also "sentence." *Cette phrase
est trop longue et manque de clarté:* this sentence is too
long and lacks clarity.

physicien. Never translate by "physician" (*docteur, méde-
cin*) but by "physicist." *Newton est le physicien à qui nous
devons les lois de la gravitation:* Newton is the physicist to
whom we owe the laws of gravity.

pièce. Like the English cognate in expressions such as "tear
to pieces" (*mettre en pièces*) or "piece of artillery" (*pièce
d'artillerie*) or "all of a piece" (*tout d'une pièce*). In addition, it also may mean "room, play." *C'est un appartement
de quatre pièces:* it is a four-room apartment. *Cette pièce
est très bien montée:* this play is very well produced. *Les
assiettes coûtent 20 frs. la pièce:* the plates are 20 frs.
each (per piece).

la pièce de résistance: the featured dish, the principal
dish

piece: *morceau.* Would you like a piece of cake? : *voulez-vous un morceau de gâteau?*

place. In addition to English meanings of "place," it is also the word for "job, seat, room, Square (*Place Vendôme*)." *Si vous continuez à travailler d'une façon si médiocre, vous finirez par perdre votre place:* if you continue working in such a mediocre way, you will end up by losing your job. *Cette place est réservée:* this seat is reserved. *Je regrette, mais il n'y a plus de place pour vos valises dans ce wagon:* I am sorry but there is no room left for your valises in this car. *J'ai acheté une voiture à deux places:* I bought a two-seater.

Place! Faites place!: make way!

faire place à quelqu'un: to make room for someone

En place! A vos places!: take your seats!

retenir des places: to secure seats

remettre quelqu'un à sa place (colloq.) : to put someone in his place

ne pas pouvoir rester en place: to be unable to keep still

bureau de placement: employment agency

plan. "Plan" in the sense of "map" or "chart." It may also mean "level, plane, ground." *Il faudra que j'achète un plan de Paris:* I shall have to buy a map of Paris. *Arrière-plan:* background. *Premier plan:* foreground.

rester en plan (colloq.) : to remain alone

laisser quelqu'un en plan (colloq.) : to leave someone in the lurch

plan (of action) : *projet, dessin*

plat. Never translate by "plate" (*assiette*) but by "dish" (both the receptacle itself and what is in it, i.e., course of a meal). *Voilà un plat digne de compliments:* this is a dish that deserves compliments.

plat du jour: main course, daily special

poser. Much wider in use and application than its English equivalent. In addition to "to pose," it may mean "to put, place, lay down, establish, suppose." *Posez donc votre paquet sur le canapé:* do lay down your package on the sofa. *Posons ce problème:* let us consider this problem.

poser des questions: to ask questions

potable. English also has the word "potable" but it is not very much used and is replaced by the ordinary word "drinkable." In French, however, *potable* is an ordinary word and you may find in stations, taps marked *eau potable* (drinking water).

prescription. It may mean "prescription (medical)" but that is a learned word in French and not too commonly used. The ordinary equivalent of it is *ordonnance.* I am going to the drugstore to get the prescription the doctor gave me for my cough: *je vais à la pharmacie chercher l'ordonnance que le docteur m'a donnée pour ma toux.*

préserver. It means "to preserve" only in the sense of "to keep safe." *Le ciel m'en préserve!:* heaven protect me!

to preserve (to keep, put into cans): *conserver, confire*

presser. In addition to the English "to press," it also means "to squeeze, crush, hurry, be urgent." *Ça ne presse pas:* there is no hurry about it. *Voulez-vous le faire tout de* *suite, nous sommes pressés:* will you please do it at once, we are in a hurry. *Pendant que vous pressez les oranges, je vais préparer du café:* I will prepare some coffee while you are squeezing the oranges.

prétendre. Never translate by "to pretend" except when the context shows that it is used in the sense of "to pretend to (lay claim to)." Usually, *prétendre* means "to say, state, affirm, maintain." *Elle prétend que cette histoire n'est pas vraie:* she claims that this story is not true. *Vous prétendez donc qu'elle n'a que quinze ans:* so you say she is only fifteen years old.

prétendu (adj.) : so-called, would-be. *C'est un prétendu génie:* he is a so-called genius.

prétendu (noun) : suitor

to pretend: *feindre, faire semblant de.* She pretended to be asleep: *elle faisait semblant de dormir.*

procès. Do not translate by "process." It is a legal term meaning "lawsuit, trial, case, action." *Je lui ai fait un procès à la suite de l'accident:* I brought action against him following the accident. *Elle a gagné son procès:* she won her case.

procès-verbal: minutes (of a meeting), statement. *Les procès-verbaux en anglais et en français de la séance seront prêts demain matin:* the English and French minutes of the meeting will be ready tomorrow morning.

process: *procédé.* What process did you use to dye your dress? : *quel procédé avez-vous employé pour teindre votre robe?*

procureur. Do not translate by "procurer," although the feminine (*procureuse*) does mean, in colloquial language, "procuress, bawd." It is usually a legal term meaning "proxy, attorney."

professeur. "Professor" as in English, but the title is applicable to any schoolmaster (except a primary school teacher who is called *instituteur, institutrice, or maître*) and to any private teacher. *Mon professeur de danse m'a dit que je faisais des progrès:* my dancing teacher told me I was improving. *Son professeur d'histoire n'est pas du tout satisfait de son travail:* his history teacher is not at all satisfied with his work.

propre. Never means "proper" except in the sense of "proper noun" (*nom propre*). When *propre* appears before a noun, it means "own." *Et dire que ma propre soeur me l'a caché!:* to think that my own sister hid it from me! When appearing after the noun, *propre* means "clean, characteristic." *Si la cuisine avait été plus propre, j'aurais loué l'appartement:* if the kitchen had been cleaner, I would have rented the apartment.

   c'est un propre à rien: he is a good-for-nothing
   le propre et le figuré: the literal and figurative sense
   proper: *exact, convenable, correct*. I don't think that it is proper for you to remain seated: *je ne crois pas qu'il soit correct que vous restiez assis*.

prune. "Plum." Our "prune" is *pruneau*.

quai. In addition to the meaning of its English equivalent, it is also the word used for "railway platform" and "lakeside promenade." *Vous pourrez acheter des journaux et des fruits sur le quai pendant l'arrêt du train:* you will be able to buy newspapers and fruits on the platform during the train stop. *Le train est à quai:* the train is in.

quart. Usually "fourth, quarter" rather than English "quart." *Donnez-moi un quart Perrier:* give me a small bottle of Perrier (a carbonated mineral water).

passer un mauvais quart d'heure: to have a bad time

For the equivalent of English "quart" see Section IV: Measurements.

quitter. Has same meaning as English "to quit" but is better translated by "to leave"; other meanings are "to give up, forsake, resign, lay aside, take off." *Qui quitte la partie la perd:* he who leaves the game loses (proverb). *Ne la quittez pas des yeux, parce qu'elle est capable de tout:* don't take your eyes off her because she is capable of anything. *J'ai quitté ma place car j'en avais assez:* I left my job because I had enough of it.

race. This word never means "race" in the sense of "competitive run" (*course*). It is "race" in the sense of "breed, strain." *C'est une belle race de chevaux:* this is a handsome breed of horses (and not a beautiful horse race). *La race jaune prédomine en Asie:* the yellow race is predominant in Asia. *Un cheval de race:* a thoroughbred horse.

raisin. Not "raisin" (*raisin sec*) but "grape." *C'est une belle grappe de raisins:* this is a nice bunch of grapes.

rapport. Sometimes may be the equivalent of "report" but it also has a variety of other meanings, the most common of which are "bearing, productiveness (of plants, etc.), respect, touch, communication, proportion, ratio, comparison." *Nos vignes sont en plein rapport:* our vines are very productive. *C'est une personne qui, sous tous les rapports, peut être considérée honnête:* this is a person who can be considered honest in every respect. *Ça fait dix ans que je ne suis plus en rapport avec Julie:* I have not been in touch with Julia for the past ten years. *Je ne vois pas de rapport entre les deux incidents:* I see no connection between the two occurrences. *Bien sûr, par rapport à ce que je gagnais il y a cinq ans, je suis aujourd'hui un homme riche:* of course, in comparison to what I earned five years ago, I am a rich man today.

raser. Besides having the English meaning of "to raze," it also means "to shave." *Je dois me raser deux fois par jour:* I have to shave twice a day.

Note that colloquially *raser* means "to bore" and *rasoir* ("razor") means a "bore."

réaliser. In French it means "to realize" only in the sense of "to make money" or "to carry out, fulfill." Otherwise use *se rendre compte. Il a réalisé des bénéfices enormes pendant la guerre:* he made huge profits during the war. *Vous rendez-vous compte qu'il est déjà minuit?:* do you realize that it is already midnight?

recevoir. In addition to having the English meaning of "to receive," it may also be translated by "to entertain, be at home." *Nous recevons tous les jeudis:* we are at home every Thursday.

Note also the following uses:

être reçu à un examen: to pass an examination

être reçu avocat: to be admitted to the bar

être reçu premier: to come out first

réclamer. Not "to reclaim" (*réformer*) nor "to reclaim land" (*défricher*), but "to complain, appeal against." *Il a réclamé auprès des autorités:* he complained to the authorities.

Note that *réclame* means "publicity, advertisement." *Ce produit est très en demande depuis qu'on en fait la réclame:* this product is in great demand since it has been advertised.

reconnaissance. Besides having the military sense of its cognate, this word also means "gratitude, recognition." *Vous pourrez toujours compter sur ma reconnaissance:* you will always be able to count on my gratitude.

regarder. This is the ordinary word for "to look at." *Qu'est-ce que vous regardez?:* what are you looking at?

Note also the following expressions:

il n'y regarde pas de si près: he is not as particular as all that

cela ne vous regarde pas: it is no concern of yours

with regard to: *quant à.* With regard to possible consequences, I will consider myself responsible: *quant aux conséquences éventuelles, je m'en rendrai responsable.*

régime. In addition to its political sense, it also has several other uses, the most common being "diet." *Le docteur l'a* *mise à un régime très sévère:* the doctor has put her on a very strict diet.

rein. Not "rein" (*rêne, guide*) but "kidneys" specifically, and "back" generally speaking. *J'ai mal aux reins:* I have a backache. *Elle a une infection aux reins:* she has a kidney infection. However, when ordering kidneys in a restaurant or butcher shop, say *rognons*.

remarquer. Sometimes "to remark" but more often "to notice." *As-tu remarqué qu'elle avait très mauvaise mine?:* did you notice that she looked very bad?

remettre. In addition to "to remit" it also means "to wear again, postpone, put back." *Je n'ai pas remis cette robe depuis l'année dernière:* I have not worn that dress again since last year. *Remets ce livre à sa place:* put that book back in its place. *Remettons cette affaire à demain:* let us put this matter off until tomorrow.

rente. Not "rent" (*loyer*) but "revenue, yearly income." *Cette maison lui donne cent mille francs de rente:* this house gives him an income of one hundred thousand francs.

Note that *rentier*, likewise, means not "renter" (*locataire*) but "person of independent means, stockholder." *Il n'a pas besoin de travailler parce qu'il est rentier:* he does not have to work because he has an income.

représentation. Not only "representation" but also "performance (of a play)." *Hier soir au théâtre, la représentation a été excellente:* last night at the theater, the performance was excellent.

However, *frais de représentation* means "expenses of official entertainment."

rester. Do not translate by "to rest." It means "to remain, stay." *Il fait trop froid pour sortir, je vais rester à la maison:* it is too cold to go out, I am going to stay home. *Je suis resté debout pendant la cérémonie:* I remained standing during the ceremony.

to rest: *se reposer.* Stay here and rest up a bit: *restez ici et reposez-vous un peu.*

The noun *reste* never means "rest" (*repos*) but "remainder, leftovers." *On va donner les restes du repas au chien:* we will give the leftovers of the meal to the dog.

résumer. Not "to resume" (*reprendre*) but "to sum up, to recapitulate, to summarize." *Voulez-vous résumer pour moi le discours du Président?:* would you summarize the President's speech for me?

réunion. Sometimes it means, as in English, "reunion" but it is also the usual word for "meeting, social gathering." *J'ai assisté à une réunion de professeurs:* I attended a teachers' meeting.

rigueur. "Rigor" as in English, but it is also used in the following expressions.

à la rigueur: if need be

être de rigueur: to be indispensable, be compulsory. *L'habit sera de rigueur:* evening dress will be required.

robe. Hardly ever translated by "robe" except when speaking of lawyers' gowns. Generally means "dress." *Voulez-vous voir la robe que je vais porter ce soir au bal?:* would you like to see the dress which I am going to wear to the ball tonight?

roman. Do not translate by "Roman" (*romain*). It means "novel, romance." *Ce roman est un des meilleurs que j'aie jamais lu:* this is one of the best novels I have ever read.

    le roman, les romans: prose fiction

    roman policier: detective story

romance. Not "romance" (*roman, affaire d'amour, affaire de coeur*) but "ballad, love song." *Les troubadours chantaient leurs romances pendant des heures:* the troubadours used to sing their ballads for hours.

    romance languages: *langues romanes*

romanesque. Sometimes "Romanesque" (Roman architectural style) but usually "romantic." *Les jeunes filles sont souvent romanesques à l'âge de vingt ans:* twenty-year-old girls are often romantic.

rose. "Pink" as well as "rose."

route. In addition to "route" also "road, path." *Ils sont en train de reconstruire la route:* they are rebuilding the road.

    grande route, route nationale: main road, highway

    se mettre en route: to set out

    frais de route: travelling expenses

    en route!: off you go! let's go!

    faire route avec quelqu'un: to travel with someone

    faire fausse route: to be on the wrong track

    rout: *déroute.* Our army put their troops to rout: *notre armée a mis leurs troupes en déroute.*

rude. Never "rude" (*mal élevé, grossier, impoli*) but "uncouth, rough, hard." *La mort de sa mère a été une rude* *épreuve:* his mother's death was a hard trial. *Les paysans de cette contrée sont souvent rudes:* the peasants in this region are often uncouth.

rudement (colloq.) : very. *Ta nouvelle bagnole est rudement chic:* your new car is awfully smart.

sable. This word may mean "sable" (both the animal and the fur, although *martre* for the former and *zibeline* for the latter are more usual) but it is also the common translation of "sand, gravel." *Le sable sur cette plage n'est pas très propre:* the sand on this beach is not too clean. *J'ai du sable dans les yeux:* I am sleepy (cf. English "the sandman").

sac. In addition to meaning "sack" it is the ordinary word for "pocketbook." *J'ai perdu mon sac:* I have lost my pocketbook.

Note a few interesting expressions with *sac:*

l'affaire est dans le sac: it's in the bag

sac à vin: boozer

avoir le sac: to be rich

prendre quelqu'un dans le sac: to catch someone red-handed

vider le sac: to unbosom oneself

sacré. As English "sacred," but like the English adjective "blessed" it is often used in the opposite sense and comes to mean "confounded, blasted." *Ce sacré mauvais temps!:* this confounded bad weather!

sage. "Sage" but, unlike the English cognate, it is often used in speaking of or to children, and means "good." *Si tu* *es sage, tu iras au cinéma:* if you are good, you will go to the movies. *C'est un enfant très sage:* he is a very good child.

salaire. Applies to "wages" of manual workers, while a white collar worker's salary is *appointements* or *traitement.*

salut. Besides "salute," it means "salvation, safety" or "bow." *Il m'a fait un profond salut:* he made me a low bow.

Salut is also used as a greeting between intimate friends, both on arrival and on leavetaking. *Salut, Pierrot, comment ça va?:* hi, Pete, how are you?

Note also the proverb *A bon entendeur, salut:* a word to the wise is sufficient.

séance. May be used in the English sense of a spiritual "seance," but it has also much more extensive use as "sitting, session, meeting." *Le tribunal est en séance:* the court is in session. *Le président a declaré la séance ouverte:* the president has opened the meeting. *Il a peint mon portrait en dix séances:* he painted my portrait in ten sittings.

sens. Not only "sense," but also "direction." On French roads, at entrance of one-way streets, you will find sign saying *sens unique* ("one way") and at exit there will be a sign reading *sens interdit* ("no entrance").

sensible. Never "sensible" (*sensé, raisonnable*), but "sensitive, susceptible, impressionable." *Il faut être gentil avec lui, car c'est un enfant très sensible:* one must be kind to him, for he is a very sensitive child. *Je suis sensible au froid:* I feel the cold (I am susceptible to the cold).

toucher la note sensible: to appeal to the emotions

67

sentence. A "court sentence" only. Otherwise it means "maxim, proverb." Use *phrase* for a "sentence" in rhetoric.

sérieux. Broader in meaning than "serious." It also means "sincere, trustworthy, honest, reliable." *C'est une maison très sérieuse:* it is a very reliable firm. *Je peux vous assurer que c'est un jeune homme très sérieux:* I can assure that he is a very trustworthy young man.

siège. Besides its military sense, as in English, it means "seat, office." *Prenez un siège:* take a seat.

   siège social: main office
   Saint-Siège: Holy See

   Note that *siège* may be used colloquially for *derrière*.

signaler. Not only "to signal" but also "to point out, to describe." *Je lui ai signalé le passage en question dans le livre:* I pointed out to him the passage in question in the book.

singe. "Monkey" and not the process of burning the end of one's hair. The verb *singer* means not "to singe" (*roussir*) but "to imitate." *J'ai singé mon professeur:* I mimicked my teacher.

slave. Not "slave" (*esclave*) but "Slav, Slavic." *Les bulgares sont des slaves:* Bulgarians are Slavs.

smoking. Oddly enough, this apparent Anglicism means "dinner-jacket, tuxedo." *Le smoking sera de rigueur:* dinner jackets will be obligatory.

société. As English "society" but also, in commercial language, "company, partnership." *C'est une société qui a fait banqueroute:* this is a company which went into bankruptcy. *Société anonyme* is the French equivalent of the

English "Limited Liability Company" (Ltd.) and of the American "Incorporated" (Inc.).

sombre. Not only "somber" but also "dark" in a physical sense, particularly of colors and the weather. *Les robes sombres me vont mieux:* I look better in dark-colored dresses. *Qu'il fait sombre ce soir!:* how dark it is tonight!

sort. Not "sort" but "fate." *Le sort n'a pas été clément pour elle:* fate was not kind to her.

tirer au sort: to draw lots

sort: *genre, espèce.* I don't like this sort of treatment at all: *ce genre de traitement ne me plaît pas du tout.*

sot. Do not translate by "sot" (*ivrogne, soûlard*) but by "fool." *Ne perdons pas notre temps avec lui, c'est un sot:* let us not waste any time with him, he is a fool.

soûl. Means "drunken" and not "soul" (*âme*). *Il est soûl comme une grive:* he is as drunk as a lord.

However, *manger son soûl* means "to eat one's fill."

souvenir. Besides "souvenir," it also means "reminder, recollection, memory." *Pour moi, j'ai un souvenir très vif du temps où j'étais un très petit enfant:* as for me, I have a very vivid recollection of the time when I was a very little child.

se souvenir: to remember, to bear in mind. *S'il m'en souvient bien, elle était très jolie:* If I recollect rightly, she was very pretty.

spectacle. Not "spectacles" (*lunettes*) but "scene, show, sight, play, entertainment." *Le lever du soleil est souvent un beau spectacle:* sunrise is often a beautiful sight.

salle de spectacle: theater

station. When it has the same meaning as the English equivalent, it applies only to small railway stations, cab stands or subway stations. Large railway stations are called *gares*.

Station may also mean "(vacation) resort."

stationner. This word, in addition to "to station," may also mean "to park, make a stop." *Nous allons stationner la voiture:* we will park the car.

stationnement interdit or *défense de stationner:* no parking

stupéfiant. As English "stupefying," but in addition "narcotic, drug." *La vente des stupéfiants devrait être interdite:* the sale of drugs ought to be forbidden.

suite. Not a "suite (of rooms)" (*appartement*) nor a "suit (of clothes)" (*complet*) but "sequel, continuation, consequence." *Suite au prochain numéro:* to be continued in our next issue. *Il est mort des suites d'une blessure:* he died of a wound.

sans suite: incoherent

supplier. Not "to supply" (*fournir*) but "to beg, to beseech." *Je l'ai supplié de me laisser partir:* I begged him to let me go.

spirituel. This word can mean "spiritual" but its most frequent meaning is "witty, humorous." *Cet homme est très spirituel:* this man is very witty.

sympathique. It is a very commonly used word in French and never means "sympathetic" (*compatissant*). It means, roughly, "congenial, pleasant, nice, likeable, swell" and is generally applied to persons. *C'est un garçon bien sym-*

pathique: he is a swell guy. *Vous nous êtes très sympathique:* we are very fond of you.

tarif. In addition to "tariff," it also means "scale of charges, rates."

   tarif télégraphique: telegraph rates
   plein tarif: adult fare, full fare
   billet à demi-tarif: half-fare ticket

tissu. Except when it means "tissue" in a medical or very general sense, this word means "textile, fabric, material." *J'ai acheté du très beau tissu avec lequel je vais me faire un manteau:* I bought some very beautiful material with which I am going to make a coat.

toilette. Besides having the sense of its English equivalent "toilet," it is also a common word for "dress." *Elle aime trop la toilette:* she is overly fond of dress.

   être en toilette: to be dressed up
   en grande toilette: in full dress
   faire sa toilette: to dress

ton. Means "tone" but also "shade." *Ces tons de gris sont ravissants:* those shades of grey are charming.

   However, a "ton" (measure of weight) is *tonne.*

toucher. Not only "to touch," but also "to play (a musical instrument), be paid, draw one's salary, cash a check, collect a bill." *Elle touche du piano:* she plays the piano. *Je touche mes appointements chaque vendredi:* I am paid every Friday. *C'est aujourd'hui que le tailleur doit venir toucher sa note:* it is today that the tailor is to collect his bill.

toucher à: to draw near, to approach, to be very close. *L'hiver touche à sa fin:* winter is drawing to an end.

touchez là! (colloq.): here's my hand on it, shake! (offer your hand while saying it)

tour. In addition to "tour" (excursion, trip), it may also mean "turn, trick." *C'est mon tour de payer:* it is my turn to pay. *Il m'a joué un mauvais tour:* he played a nasty trick on me.

In the feminine, *tour* means "tower." *La tour Eiffel:* the Eiffel Tower.

translation. Never render by "translation" (*traduction*). It means "transferral."

transpirer. Besides meaning "to transpire," it is the ordinary term for "to perspire." *La partie de tennis l'a fait beaucoup transpirer:* the tennis match made him perspire a great deal.

tuteur. Not "tutor" (*précepteur*) but "guardian, trustee." *Elle vit avec son tuteur depuis que ses parents sont morts:* she has lived with her guardian since the death of her parents.

type. Not only "type" but also colloquial term for "character, fellow." *C'est un type très courageux:* he is a very brave fellow. *Quel type!:* what a guy!

unique. Does not always have the English meaning of "unique." Is often used in the sense of "only, single." *Il est fils unique:* he is an only son. *Sens unique:* one-way street.

Vous êtes unique! (colloq.): you are the limit!

vacation. This is a rather uncommon word in French, meaning "recess (of law-courts)." Translate "vacation" by *vacances*.

vaisselle. Do not render by "vessel" (*vaisseau, navire*). The meaning of this word is the more prosaic "dishes, table service." *Y a-t-il qui que ce soit qui aime faire la vaisselle?:* is there anyone at all who likes to wash dishes?

valable. Not "valuable" (*précieux, de grande valeur*) but "valid, good." *Mon billet est valable pour deux mois:* my ticket is good for two months. *Il faudra que j'invente une excuse valable pour éviter d'aller à ce dîner:* I will have to make up a valid excuse to avoid going to that dinner.

veille. Never means "veil" but "eve, watch, vigil." *J'ai dû faire de longues veilles pour passer cet examen:* I had to stay up many long nights in order to pass this examination. *Je l'ai vu la veille de Noël:* I saw him on Christmas Eve.
veil: *voile*. The bride's veil was made out of lace: *le voile de la mariée était en dentelle.*

vilain. In modern French, this word does not mean "villainous" (*vil, infâme, scélérat*) but "ugly, shabby, naughty, unpleasant, sordid." *Oh, la vilaine!:* for shame, you naughty girl! *C'est un vilain moment à passer:* this is a nasty moment to go through. *Quelle vilaine rue!:* what an awful street!

vue. Not only "view" but also "sight, eyesight." *Si tu ne portes pas tes lunettes, tu perdras la vue:* if you won't wear your eyeglasses, you will lose your sight.

personnes les plus en vue: persons most in the public eye

à perte de vue: as far as the eye can reach

vulgariser. Means "to popularize" as well as "to vulgarize."
Il est l'auteur d'un ouvrage de vulgarisation de médecine:
he is the author of a popular treatise on medicine.

wagon (pronounced *vagon*). This is the regular word for
"railway car."

wagon-lit: sleeping car
wagon-restaurant: diner

II. WHAT YOU DIDN'T LEARN
IN SCHOOL

Important and useful vocabulary and expressions not included in most school texts

à. Some frequent uses:

à moi; à vous: it's my turn; it's your turn

Je suis à vous: at your service. For example, in a shop a saleslady who is busy with another customer may say to you: *Je suis à vous dans un moment:* I'll be with you in a moment.

abruti: fool, stupid, stupid person.

abrutissant: stupefying. *C'est un travail abrutissant:* it's stupefying work.

accomoder. *Il s'accomode de tout:* he is easy to please.

âge. *Prendre de l'âge:* to be getting on in years.

l'âge ingrât: the awkward age (adolescence)

être dans la force de l'âge: to be in the prime of life

être entre deux âges: to be middle-aged

le moyen âge: the Middle Ages

argot: slang. *Il est désirable d'avoir quelques notions d'argot pour comprendre le français tel qu'on le parle aujourd'hui:* it is desirable to have some knowledge of slang in order to understand French as it is spoken today.

assommant: boring. *Le nouveau professeur est assommant:* the new teacher is a terrible bore.

avis. *Sauf avis contraire:* unless I hear (or write) to the contrary.

banlieue: suburbs. *St. Cloud fait partie de la banlieue de Paris:* St. Cloud is part of the Paris suburbs. In railroad stations, the sign *Banlieue* indicates the platform for the suburban trains.

bavard: talkative, loquacious. *Qu'elle est bavarde!:* what a chatterbox she is!

belotte. A very popular French card game, resembling pinochle, but simpler and faster.

bondé: crowded. *Les autobus sont toujours bondés à cette heure:* the buses are always crowded at this hour.

briquet: cigarette lighter. *Je n'ai pas d'allumettes, mais voici mon briquet:* I haven't any matches, but here's my lighter.

buissonnière. *Faire l'école buissonnière:* to stay away from school; to play hookey, truant.

caisse: cashier's desk. *Payez à la caisse, s'il vous plaît:* please pay the cashier.

carnet: notebook, memorandum book, check book, booklet of bus or subway tickets.

chercher. Besides "to look for," it may have several other translations:

Je viendrai vous chercher vers huit heures: I shall call for you at about eight o'clock.

Je vais chercher votre manteau: I'll go and get your coat.

Envoyez chercher ma voiture: send for my car.

chercher midi à quatorze heures: to look for difficulties where none exist *chercher femme:* to look for a wife. Compare this with the popular expression *cherchez la femme:* look for the woman; there's a woman at the bottom of this.

clôture: closing. In Paris most of the theaters close during the summer, and the *Clôture annuelle* sign is often posted.

compris: included. To ask if the tipping charge has been included in the bill, you say: *service compris?* or *le service, est-il compris?*

comptant: cash, ready money. *Au comptant:* for cash, in cash.

consigne: checkroom for baggage. *Je vais laisser mes valises à la consigne:* I'm going to check my valises.

coupe: haircut. *Je voudrais une coupe:* I would like a haircut.

courrier: mail. *Est-ce qu'il y a du courrier pour moi?:* is there any mail for me?

couvert: setting.

> *mettre le couvert:* to set the table
> *ôter le couvert:* to clear the table
> *table de cinq couverts:* table for five

dégoûtant: unpleasant, annoying. *Que c'est dégoûtant d'avoir de la pluie tous les dimanches!:* it's so annoying to have rain every Sunday!

descendre. In addition to the usual meaning of "descend, come down," the following should be noted.

> *descendre à un hôtel:* to stop at a hotel
> *Porteur, veuillez descendre mes bagages:* porter, will you please take down my baggage.

Tout le monde descend!: everybody off!

dessous. *Avoir le dessous:* to get the worst of it. Note also *avoir le dessus:* to have the upper hand.

détraqué: out of order. *La ligne est détraquée:* the line is out of order. Also used popularly in referring to persons. *Elle est tout à fait détraquée:* she's completely nuts.

douane: customs. *Il faut passer par la douane avant de quitter la gare:* you must go through customs before leaving the station.

douche: shower. *Vous pouvez prendre une douche à une des piscines à Paris:* you can take a shower at one of the swimming pools in Paris.

doux. "Quiet, tender, soft," in addition to "sweet." *J'ai la peau très douce:* I have very tender skin.

    Il fait doux: the weather is mild.

    faire les yeux doux: to cast amorous glances

    poisson d'eau douce: fresh-water fish

    un billet doux: a love letter

    tout doux: softly, gently, quietly

    Parlez doucement: speak softly.

échéant. *Le cas échéant:* if such should be the case; in that case.

écouter. *J'écoute* is frequently used over the telephone in the sense of "speaking; this is he." —*Allô, allô, je voudrais parler à Monsieur Durand.* —*J'écoute:* "Hello, I'd like to talk to Mr. Durand." "Speaking."

entendre. *Entendre raison:* to listen to reason.

    entendre à demi-mot: to take a hint

s'entendre avec quelqu'un: to come to an understanding with someone

entendu or *c'est entendu:* very well, all right, agreed, O.K. *Entendu* especially is very frequently used. *Demain nous irons au théâtre ensemble, n'est-ce pas? Entendu:* tomorrow we shall go to the theater together, won't we? O.K. *Alors, c'est entendu, tu ne partiras pas sans me prévenir:* well then, it's agreed; you'll not leave without informing me.

entr'acte: intermission.

entre. Note the following ways of saying "between ourselves, between you and me": *entre nous, entre nous soit dit, soit dit entre vous et moi.*

épuiser: to exhaust. *Cette promenade m'a épuisé:* that walk tired me out. *L'édition est épuisée:* the book is out of print.

étrenne (usually in the plural): Christmas or New Year's gift.

étrenner une robe: to wear a dress for the first time

exemple. A popular interjection which may be variously translated as "the idea! upon my word! indeed!" *Par exemple, je trouve cette idée excellente!:* indeed, this is an excellent idea! *Par exemple, je ne le ferai pas:* No, sir, I won't do it. *La pièce n'était pas très réussie, mais les costumes étaient beaux par exemple!:* the play wasn't very good, but the costumes were very beautiful indeed!

fâcheux: troublesome, inopportune, unfortunate. *Il est fâcheux que vous vous soyez trompé d'adresse:* it is unfortunate that you made a mistake in the address.

le fâcheux de l'affaire: the worst of the matter

façon. *C'est un homme sans façon:* he is easy to get on with.

On travaille à façon (a sign that may be seen in a tailor's shop): customers' own material made up

fait. *Si fait!:* yes, indeed!

Je suis sûr de mon fait: I am sure of what I am saying.

Il lui a dit son fait: he gave him a piece of his mind; he told him what he thought of him.

Faits divers is a section of a newspaper containing brief news reports.

faubourg: suburb, outskirts. In certain French cities, and especially Paris, certain districts which used to be outside the city but which today are no longer considered suburbs, have preserved the name. For example, *Faubourg St. Germain, Faubourg St. Antoine. Les faubourgs:* the working classes of these districts.

fleurette. *Conter fleurette:* to say sweet nothings.

folichon. Even though it bears a resemblance to *fol* ("mad"), it has the weaker and kinder meaning of "playful, full of fun." *Ce folichon de Pierre:* that devil of a Pierre.

fort. Frequently used instead of *très* for "very."

Ils nous ont fort bien reçus: they entertained us very well.

Il faut que j'aille lui parler, c'est plus fort que moi: I must go and speak to him, I can't help it.

gêner: to trouble, bother. *Est-ce que je vous gêne?:* am I in your way? It may also be used ironically to someone inconveniencing others. *Ne vous gênez pas!:* make yourself at home! don't mind us!

hauteur. *Etre à la hauteur:* to be equal to, able to. *J'espère être à la hauteur de la tâche que vous m'avez confiée:* I hope to be equal to the task you have entrusted to me.

heure. *A la bonne heure!:* well done! fine! *J'ai entendu que vous avez décidé de faire un voyage en France. A la bonne heure!:* I heard you have decided to take a trip to France. Splendid!

    à l'heure précise: on the dot, sharp. *Je suis arrivée à dix heures précises:* I arrived at ten o'clock sharp.

    passer un mauvais quart d'heure: to have a bad time of it. *J'ai passé un mauvais quart d'heure chez le dentiste:* I had a bad time of it at the dentist's.

importer. *Qu'importe!* or *n'importe!:* no matter! it is of no consequence.

    n'importe quoi: anything at all. *J'ai très faim et suis prêt à manger n'importe quoi:* I'm so hungry I'll eat anything.

s'inquiéter: to worry. *Ne vous inquiétez pas, je m'occuperai de tout:* don't worry, I'll take care of everything.

insu. *A mon insu:* without my knowledge.

jeu: game. *C'est vieux jeu:* that is old-fashioned.

jumelles: "Twin girls" but also "opera glasses." *Ma soeur vient d'avoir des jumelles:* my sister just had twin girls. *J'ai prêté mes jumelles à ma soeur:* I lent my opera glasses to my sister.

klaxon: horn (of automobile). *Sonnez le klaxon:* blow the horn.

lavabo: toilet; washstand.

libre: unoccupied. *Est-ce que cette place est libre?:* is this seat unoccupied?

lors de: at the time of, during. *N'y êtes-vous pas allé lors de votre dernier séjour en Europe?:* didn't you go there during your last trip to Europe?

lourd. Besides "heavy" it may also mean "dull-witted, stupid."

madame. In speaking to servants, waiters, etc., one refers to one's wife as *madame. Pour moi la soupe à l'oignon et pour madame un consommé:* I'll have the onion soup and my wife will have a consommé.

  Madame est servie (set phrase): dinner is served

  See also Section IV, "French Courtesy."

mademoiselle. In addition to meaning "young lady, miss," it is the proper word for addressing a waitress, saleslady, telephone operator, etc.

maillot: bathing suit. Used much more frequently than *costume de bain.*

main. *Donner un coup de main:* to give a helping hand.

  J'en mettrais la main au feu: I would stake my life on it.

  tenir une nouvelle de bonne main: to have a piece of news on good authority

mairie: town hall.

malheur: bad luck, misfortune. *Par malheur:* as ill luck would have it.

Je l'ai appris pour mon malheur: I found out about it to my sorrow.

jouer de malheur: to have a run of bad luck, be unlucky

manquer. A very useful verb with many possible translations.

Il manque du sel à cette soupe: this soup needs salt.

Je ne manque de rien: I don't need anything.

Vous nous manquerez: we shall miss you.

Il ne manquait plus que cela!: that was the last straw!

Il s'en manque de beaucoup: far from it.

manquer à sa parole: to break one's word

C'est un garçon manqué (colloq.) : she's a tomboy.

marchander: to bargain.

marché. *Marché conclu est marché conclu:* a bargain is a bargain.

même. *A même de:* in a position to, able to. *Il est à même de vous entendre:* he is able to hear you.

mercerie: notions store; haberdashery.

merci. When thanking someone you usually say *merci bien* or, less frequently, *merci beaucoup. Merci,* when used alone, may mean "no, thank you" in declining an offer. *Veux-tu que je t'envoie de ce parfum? —Merci, j'en ai encore deux bouteilles:* do you wish me to send you some of this perfume? No, thank you, I still have two bottles. (See Section IV on French Courtesy.)

mieux. *Je ne demande pas mieux:* nothing would give me greater pleasure.

faute de mieux: for want of anything better. *Faute de mieux, je passerai mes vacances en ville:* for want of something better, I shall spend my vacation in the city.

mignon: cute, pretty. *Votre bébé est tellement mignon:* your baby is so cute.

moins. *Pas le moins du monde:* not a bit; not in the slightest.

monsieur. (See Section IV, "French Courtesy.") Note also its use in addressing a person with a title. *M. le maire:* Mr. Mayor. In very polite language, *monsieur, madame* or *mademoiselle* may be used in referring to a relative of the person addressed. *Et monsieur votre père, il va toujours bien?:* and your father is well, I trust. Servants often use the third person form of address. *Le bain de monsieur est prêt:* your bath is ready, sir.

Note the expression *faire le monsieur:* to put on airs, act like a big shot. The feminine equivalent is *faire la grande dame.*

moyen. *Il n'y a pas moyen (de faire cela):* it can't be done.

navette. *Faire la navette:* to go to and fro between two places. *Mon travail m'oblige à faire la navette entre Marseille et Paris tous les mois:* my work obliges me to shuttle between Marseilles and Paris every month.

navré: dreadfully sorry, brokenhearted. *J'ai été navrée d'apprendre que vous étiez à l'hôpital:* I was dreadfully sorry to learn that you were in the hospital.

nécessaire. *Faire le nécessaire:* to take care of everything, see to it. *Ne vous préoccupez pas, je ferai tout le néces-*

saire: don't trouble yourself, I'll take care of everything.

nuit. *Passer une nuit blanche:* to spend a sleepless night; not to sleep a wink.

outrance. *Une guerre à outrance:* a war to the death.

panne: breakdown, mishap, delay (on subway), failure (of electricity). *J'ai déjà eu trois pannes avec cette voiture:* I've already had three breakdowns with this car.

　　laisser quelqu'un en panne (colloq.): to leave someone in the lurch.

pardon. (See Section IV, "French Courtesy.") When approaching strangers it is polite to say *pardon, monsieur (madame, mademoiselle)*, before asking your question. *Pardon, madame, où est la rue de Rivoli?:* excuse me, where is rue de Rivoli?

parole. *Avoir la parole:* to have the floor.

part. *Vous venez de la part de qui?:* you come through whom, on whose recommendation?

patois: dialect. *Beaucoup de provinces en France ont leur propre patois:* many French provinces have their own dialects.

pays. In addition to "country," it also means "district, region." *Je ne sais pas quelle est la meilleure route parce que je ne suis pas du pays:* I don't know which is the best route because I'm not from this district.

pelouse: lawn, grass. *Défense de se promener sur la pelouse:* keep off the grass.

piéton: pedestrian. *Les passages cloutés sont réservés aux piétons:* the nailed lanes are reserved for pedestrians.

perdre. *Je m'y perds:* I cannot make head or tail of it.

plaisir. *Au plaisir* is one of the common, though formal, substitutions for *au revoir.*

plaît-il?: I beg your pardon (on not hearing something).

prendre. *A tout prendre:* on the whole, everything considered. *A tout prendre, c'est une plutôt jolie ville:* on the whole, it's a rather pretty town.

C'est à prendre ou à laisser: take it or leave it.

s'y prendre mal: to do something the wrong way. *Vous vous y prenez mal; c'est comme ça qu'il faut le faire:* you're doing it all wrong; it should be done like this.

On ne m'y prendra pas (colloq.): I won't fall for it; I know better.

pris: taken, seized, captured, busy. *Je regrette, mais je suis prise ce soir:* I'm sorry but I'm busy tonight. *Cette place est déjà prise:* this seat is already taken.

prier. *Je vous prie:* please. *Asseyez vous, je vous prie:* please sit down.

Je vous en prie may mean both "please" and "you're welcome." *Vous permettez que je fume?—Je vous en prie:* may I smoke? Please do. *Merci bien.—Je vous en prie:* thank you very much. You're welcome.

propos. *Changer de propos:* to change the subject. *Changeons de propos:* let's talk about something else.

province: province. *En province:* in the provinces, in the country, away from Paris. *Tu ne peux t'imaginer comme c'est merveilleux d'être de retour à Paris après toutes ces* *années passées en province:* you can't imagine how wonderful it is to be back in Paris after all these years in the provinces.

Provence is an ancient province of southeastern France which includes the famous *Côte d'Azur* or *Riviera.* (The French always say *Côte d'Azur.*)

quand même: nevertheless, in spite of all. *Je le ferai quand même:* I'll do it in spite of all; I'll do it all the same. *Tout en étant différant de la dernière fois, c'était quand même très agréable:* while it was quite different from the last time, it was nevertheless very pleasant.

quoi. *A quoi bon?:* what's the use?

un je ne sais quoi: a certain something, an undefinable quality. *Elle avait un je ne sais quoi de charmant:* she had an undefinable charm.

radiodiffuser: to broadcast. *Le discours du Président va certainement être radiodiffusé:* the President's speech will surely be broadcast.

raffoler: to be very fond of. *Je raffole de bananes:* I'm very fond of bananas. *Je n'en raffole pas:* I'm not crazy (or wild) about it.

raison. *A plus forte raison* or *raison de plus:* all the more reason.

ralentir: to slow down. *Il faut ralentir aux tournants:* one must slow down on curves.

ravissant: pretty, ravishing. *Vous êtes ravissante ce soir:* you are bewitching tonight.

relâche: respite, rest. It appears sometimes on weekly programs of theaters and means that the theater is closed for that particular evening.

rendez-vous. *Prendre rendez-vous:* to make an appointment. *Donner rendez-vous à quelqu'un:* to make an appointment with someone. *Se donner rendez-vous:* to agree to meet.

renseignements: information.

service. *A votre service:* at your service; you're welcome. *Je vous remercie, monsieur, de m'avoir accompagnée jusqu'ici. —A votre service, madame:* thank you for having accompanied me here. You're welcome.

   escalier de service: back stairs

serviette: towel, napkin. It may also mean "briefcase, portfolio." *L'avocat portait ses documents dans sa serviette:* the lawyer was carrying his documents in his briefcase.

si. When a question is asked negatively, the answer in the affirmative should be *si,* not *oui. Tu n'as pas encore acheté les disques? —Mais si, hier:* you haven't bought the records yet? Yes, indeed, yesterday.

solde: clearance sale, bargains. *Nous avons des bas en solde:* we have stockings or sale.

stylo. Abbreviation of *stylographe,* "fountain pen." *Stylo* is used much more frequently than *plume.*

sûr. *Bien sûr:* of course, sure. *Est-ce que tu viendras me visiter à l'hôpital? —Mais bien sûr:* will you come and visit me at the hospital? But of course. *Bien sûr, je le ferai:* of course I'll do it.

tenir. *Tenir à faire quelque chose:* to be bent on doing something; to be anxious to do something.

tenir quelque chose de bonne source: to have something on good authority

tort. *Parler à tort et à travers:* to talk at random, without rhyme or reason.

tout. An extremely versatile adverb meaning "very, quite, wholly, entirely, thoroughly."

Elle était tout émue: she was quite moved.

Je suis tout à vous: I am at your service (*or* disposal).

C'est tout près d'ici: It is quite near here.

tout beau or *tout doux:* softly, gently, not so fast

tout à coup: suddenly

tout d'un coup: all at once

tout de bon: in earnest

tout au moins: at least

tout à fait: quite, entirely

tout de suite: immediately

C'est tout un: it is all the same. *Aller à la campagne ou rester en ville, c'est tout un pour moi:* to go to the country or to stay in town, it's all the same to me.

trop. *Etre de trop:* to be in the way; to be unwelcome.

trouver. *Vous trouvez?:* you think so?

vedette: star (actor or actress). *La grande vedette est en train de distribuer des autographes:* the great star is giving out autographs.

vestiaire: cloakroom (in restaurants, theaters, etc.) *Je vais laisser mon manteau au vestiaire:* I am going to leave my coat in the cloakroom. *Apportez-moi mon vestiaire ici:* bring my things here from the cloakroom.

voir. *Ceci est à voir, c'est à voir* and *c'est ce que nous verrons* are all equivalent to the English "that remains to be seen" or "we shall see what we shall see."

voiture. The general word for "vehicle," similar to our "car" (automobile or train).

En voiture!: all aboard!

volonté. *A volonté:* at will, at pleasure. *Vous aurez de l'argent à volonté:* you'll have money whenever you want it.

volontiers: gladly, willingly, with pleasure. *Voulez-vous m'accompagner à la gare? Volontiers:* would you like to come to the station with me? Gladly. *Je le ferai très volontiers:* I'll do it with great pleasure.

III. THE GALLIC FLAVOR

The most popular slang and colloquial expressions necessary to understand French "as it is spoke."

à. Sometimes used incorrectly in place of *de* to express possession. *Le vélo à mon frère:* my brother's bike.

accoucher. The literal meaning of "to give birth to" has been extended in the slang use of the word, and means "to utter with difficulty (after coaxing or persuasion), to cough up." *Allons, accouche, mon vieux:* come now, out with it, old man. *Je ne réussis pas à accoucher de cette dissertation:* I just don't seem to be able to get through with this dissertation.

agacer: to irritate, annoy, get on one's nerves. *N'agace pas ce chien, ou il finira par te mordre:* don't annoy that dog or he'll end up by biting you.

aller. In addition to its many correct uses, this verb is used in a number of colloquial expressions.

Comment ça va or simply *ça va* is the usual greeting among friends. *Ça va* also means "fine, O.K."

Allons donc!: come now! You're joking!

Allez-y: go to it; it's your turn.

y aller fort: to exaggerate. *Tu y vas un peu fort, mon vieux:* you're exaggerating a bit, aren't you, pal?

Elle le fait aller: she makes him do what she likes.

Cela va comme sur des roulettes: that's going smoothly.

Rien ne va plus: no more bets (in gambling houses).

au pis-aller: at the worst, as a last resort. *Au pis-aller, ils me donneront une amende:* at the worst, they'll give me a fine.

ami, amie. These innocent words for "friend" sometimes have in slang the force of *amant, maîtresse,* "lover, mistress."

amour. *Vous êtes un amour:* you're a darling. But be careful of the expression *faire l'amour* which has sexual overtones in French slang. For "to make love" say *faire la cour.*

ange. *Etre aux anges:* to be in seventh heaven.

arranger. *Arrangez-vous:* do it as best you can.

Comme vous voilà arrangé!: what a sight you are!

as: ace, first-rate, A-1. *C'est un as du tennis:* he's an excellent tennis player. *Mon frangin est un as en algèbre:* my brother is a whiz in algebra.

assiette. *Ne pas être dans son assiette:* to feel out of sorts; not to be at one's best. *Je n'étais pas dans mon assiette ce matin, et par conséquent j'ai perdu:* I wasn't at my best this morning, so I lost.

avoir. *J'en ai pour deux heures:* I shall be busy for two hours; it will take me two hours.

Votre équipe a gagné aujourd'hui, mais on vous aura: your team won today, but we'll get even with you.

baba. May refer to sponge cake usually soaked in rum. But in slang it is used as an adjective and means "astonished." *Elle en est restée baba quand elle a découvert ce qui* *s'était passé:* she was astounded when she discovered what had happened.

bac, bachot. Student slang for *baccalauréat,* the degree granted on finishing the *lycée,* roughly equivalent to American high school plus one year of college. It may also refer to the comprehensive examination given before the degree is granted. *Passer le bac:* to pass one's final *lycée* exams.

bagnole. A popular slang substitute for *automobile. Je me suis acheté une belle petite bagnole:* I bought myself a cute little car.

baiser. Avoid using this word which the dictionaries translate as "to kiss." In French slang it has come to mean "to have sexual intercourse." Use instead *embrasser. Baiser* may be used in such constructions as *il m'a baisé la main:* he kissed my hand. It is also permissible as a noun. *Je t'envoie mes plus tendres baisers:* I send you sweet kisses (ending of a love letter).

balade. Frequently used instead of *promenade* for "walk, stroll." *Faire une balade:* to take a walk, go for a stroll.

se balader: to walk, stroll. *Il fait assez chaud pour se balader à la plage:* it's warm enough to take a walk at the beach.

balai. *On lui a donné du balai:* they gave him the sack, they fired him.

balancer. In addition to its accepted uses, it appears in one of the many French slang equivalents of "I don't give a damn": *je m'en balance.*

bande. Often used in insults. *Une bande d'idiots:* a bunch of dopes.

barbe. The word for beard also means "bore, nuisance" in slang. *Quelle barbe de devoir aller à ce dîner!*: what a nuisance to have to go to that dinner! There is also the verb *barber*: to bore, annoy. *Je ne me suis jamais autant barbé qu'à la conférence d'hier soir*: I was never so bored as at last night's lecture. It is interesting to note that *rasoir*, *raseur* and *raser* have the same meanings as *barbe* and *barber*.

bécane: bike. *J'aime beaucoup aller à bécane*: I love to ride a bike.

béguin: boy friend or girl friend. *C'est mon béguin*: he's my sweetheart. *Avoir le béguin pour*: to be sweet on, have a crush on. *Il a un béguin pour Odette depuis très longtemps*: he's had a crush on Odette for a very long time.

bile. *Ne pas se faire de bile*: to take things easy.

bille: face, mug, kisser. *Il a une bonne bille*: he has an honest face. *Ce type a une sale bille*: this guy has an ugly mug.

bistro: a small restaurant. *Vous trouverez qu'en France on mange aussi bien aux bistros qu'aux restaurants de luxe*: you'll find that in France one eats as well in small eating places as in luxury restaurants.

blague: trick, joke, lie. *Son répertoire de blagues est immense*: his stock of jokes is immense. *Sans blague*: really, no kidding.

    blaguer: to joke, kid. *Allons, ne blaguez pas; parlons sérieusement*: come now, stop kidding; let's talk seriously.

bleu. In addition to describing the celestial color, *bleu* has a number of other uses.

Petit bleu (so called because of its color) is a rapid delivery letter sent by pneumatic tube in Paris.

Cordon bleu means an excellent cook, after the cooking school of that name.

peur bleue: terrible fright

Ma jambe est couverte de bleus: my leg is black and blue.

bobard (usually in the plural) : nonsense, rubbish, tall story.
Assez de bobards, maintenant racontez-nous ce qui s'est vraiment passé: enough of this nonsense, now tell us what really happened.

boîte. Literally "box," it is used by extension to mean in slang "jail, joint, mouth."
Quelle boîte!: what a place!
Ferme ta boîte!: shut up!
boîte de nuit: night club

bombe. *Faire la bombe:* to go on a spree, paint the town red. *Pour fêter mon anniversaire, on va faire la bombe:* we'll go on a spree to celebrate my birthday.

bonjour. *Facile comme bonjour:* as easy as pie. *L'examen de géometrie était facile comme bonjour:* the geometry exam was as easy as pie.

bouche. *Ta bouche!:* shut up!
faire la petite bouche: to be hard to please

bouché: stupid, thick, dense. *Il est tellement bouché que toutes vos explications seront inutiles:* he's so thick that all your explanations will be useless.

boucler: to shut. *Boucle-la!:* shut up! dry up!

bouffer. A very common substitute for *manger*, "to eat." *Si vous voulez, on peut bouffer dans le bistro au coin:* If you wish, we can eat at the little place on the corner.

bougeotte. *Avoir la bougeotte:* to be fidgety, restless. *Il a la bougeotte, alors ça ne m'étonne pas qu'il soit parti:* he can't stay in the same place, so I'm not surprised that he left.

boulot. Frequently used in place of *travail*, "work." *Il y a beaucoup de boulot au bureau ces jours-ci:* there's lots of work at the office these days.

bouquin. Literally "old book," but popularly used for "book" in general.

boustifailler: to eat a lot, stuff oneself.

brin. *Un beau brin de fille:* a fine slip of a girl.

bûcher. Commonly used among students for "to study hard, cram." *Je dois bûcher cet examen:* I must cram for this exam.

ça (contraction of *cela*) is used in numerous popular expressions.

C'est ça: that's right, all right

C'était un peu fort, ça!: that was a bit too much!

Ça y est: everything's ready; all right

Avec ça que expresses strong affirmation. *Avec ça qu'il n'est pas avare!:* don't tell me he isn't a miser! *Avec ça qu'il traite bien sa femme!:* don't imagine he treats his wife well!

C'est pas tout, ça: that's all very well; that's not the point. *C'est pas tout ça, mais il faut aussi avoir de l'argent pour acheter la maison:* that's all very well, but one must also have the money to pay for the house.

Comment ça va or *ça va?:* How are things? This is the most frequently heard greeting in the language.

Comme ci, comme ça or *couci-couça:* so-so

Ça va: all right, O.K.

cancan. In addition to being a famous dance, *cancan* may mean "scandal, gossip." *On a fait beaucoup de cancans sur le maire de cette ville:* there was a great deal of gossip about the mayor of this city.

cafard: the blues. *Je crois que le mauvais temps est la cause de mon cafard:* I think the bad weather is the reason for my feeling blue.

avoir le cafard: to have the blues. *Laissez-le tranquille, il a le cafard aujourd'hui:* leave him alone, he's feeling depressed today.

calé: to be well up in, know one's stuff. *Il est très calé en géographie:* he's very good in geography.

canard: false news, rumor. *Un canard* may also be a lump of sugar dipped in brandy or coffee.

chahut. *Faire du chahut:* to kick up a row, be very noisy.

chanter. *Si ça vous chante:* if you're in the mood for it; if you feel like it.

chat. *Avoir un chat dans la gorge:* to have a frog (literally "cat") in the throat; to be hoarse.

chaud. *Ça ne me fait ni chaud ni froid:* I don't care a bit (one way or the other).

chic. This word is current in English and correct French in the sense of "fashionable." In colloquial French it has some additional uses: "fine, swell, wonderful." *Il a été très chic avec moi:* he was very kind to me. *Ça n'est pas très chic de sa part:* it's not very nice of him.

des gens chics: stylish people

un type chic: a fashionable fellow

un chic type: a good guy, a pal

avoir du chic: to be stylish. *Ce manteau a beaucoup de chic:* this coat has a great deal of style.

Chic, nous irons à la plage demain!: wonderful, tomorrow we'll go to the beach!

chien. *Il fait un temps de chien* or *il fait un chien de temps:* the weather is awful.

se donner un mal de chien: to overwork oneself, slave away. *Je me suis donné un mal de chien pour réparer cette radio:* I worked like a dog to fix this radio.

avoir du chien: to have charm and winning ways. *Juliette n'est pas jolie, mais elle a du chien:* Juliette isn't pretty, but she has charm.

chiper: to swipe, pinch. *Quelqu'un a dû chiper mes cigarettes:* someone must have swiped my cigarettes.

chose. Frequently used when one cannot recall the name of a person or object. *Mais c'est chose qui me l'a dit!:* but it was what's-his-name who told it to me!

Bien des choses chez vous: kind regards to your family.

C'est chose faite: it's an accomplished fact.

chou. Besides meaning "cabbage," a *chou* is a kind of cream puff in the shape of a cabbage. A favorite term of endearment is *mon petit chou:* my little darling.

chouette. It is interesting to note that the word for "owl" has the slang meaning of "fine, nice, excellent." *Mon nouveau professeur d'espagnol a l'air chouette:* my new Spanish teacher seems to be very nice. *Chouette! Henri nous emmène tous au restaurant:* wonderful! Henry is taking us all out to the restaurant.

clou: chief attraction. *La danseuse espagnole a été le clou de la soirée:* the Spanish dancer was the chief attraction of the evening.

    mettre au clou: to pawn, hock. *Il faudra que je mette ma montre au clou:* I'll have to pawn my watch.

cochon. Literally "pig, swine." A very insulting term.

    jouer un tour de cochon: to play a dirty trick

coco. A term of endearment with children. Oddly enough, it may also have a pejorative meaning. *Méfiez-vous de ce coco-là:* don't trust that guy. The feminine *cocotte* likewise can mean "my little darling" and is also used for a "fast or immoral woman." Be careful not to confuse *coco* with *cocu,* "cuckold."

coeur. *Il a un coeur d'artichaut:* he falls in love (or pretends to) with every woman he meets. The simile is self-explanatory if one recalls the many leaves that may be plucked from the heart of an artichoke.

coiffé. *Etre né coiffé:* to be born with a silver spoon in one's mouth.

    coiffer Sainte Catherine: to remain an old maid (Saint Catherine being the patron saint of virgins)

combien. Note the popular ungrammatical way of asking the date: *nous sommes le combien?*

comble: limit. *Elle a refusé de vous voir? Ça, c'est le comble!:* she refused to see you? That's the limit!

comme. *C'est tout comme:* it amounts to the same thing; it's all the same.

comme tout: very much, like anything. *C'est marrant comme tout:* it's funny as can be.

copain (feminine *copine*): chum, pal, buddy. Popular slang substitute for *camarade*. *Je voudrais te présenter un vieux copain à moi:* I'd like to introduce an old pal of mine.

coucher. In slang it often implies sexual intercourse.

coup. The following are just a few of the most popular of the many expressions in which *coup* appears.

>   *du premier coup:* right away; the very first time
>   *coup de foudre:* love at first sight
>   *coup de tête:* rash action
>   *C'est un coup monté:* it's a put-up job.

courir. *Par le temps qui court:* nowadays, as times go.

cran: nerve, guts. *Il aura ses défauts, mais on ne peut pas lui reprocher de ne pas avoir du cran:* he may have his faults, but you can't say he doesn't have guts.

crémaillère. Literally "pot-hanger." *Pendre la crémaillère:* to give a house-warming party.

crevant: very funny, hilarious. *Le film que nous avons vu hier était crevant:* the picture we saw yesterday was hilarious. It may also mean "very tiring" in the physical sense. *C'est un voyage crevant:* it's an exhausting trip.

crever: burst, split, die and other possible translations. *Tu peux crever avant que je te le donne:* you can burst before I give it to you.

crever de faim: to starve

crever d'ennui: to be bored to death

Ça vous crève les yeux: it's staring you in the face.

se crever: to wear oneself out working

se crever de rire: to split one's sides laughing

cri. *Le dernier cri:* the rage, last word, latest style. *Les robes tricotées sont le dernier cri:* knitted dresses are the last word (of fashion).

croûte: food. *Casser la croûte:* to have a snack, bite. A sign outside a small restaurant may say *Casse-croûte à toutes heures:* open all day for light snacks. *Nous casserons la croûte à notre retour:* we'll have a bite on our return.

cuver. Literally, "to ferment, settle." *Cuver son vin:* to sleep oneself sober, sleep it off.

dactylo. Popular abbreviation of *dactylographe*, "typist."

dada: mania, hobby. *Mon dada à moi, c'est la photographie:* my hobby is photography. *Etre sur son dada:* to indulge in one's hobby.

danger. *Pas de danger:* not likely, not a chance. *Il n'y a pas de danger qu'il se dérange pour venir nous voir:* it's not likely that he'll trouble himself to come and see us. *Allez-vous lui demander pardon? —Pas de danger!:* are you going to ask him to forgive you? —Not a chance!

débrouillard: resourceful, able to shift for oneself.

se débrouiller: to get along O.K. (by oneself), manage. *Je n'ai pas beaucoup d'argent, mais je pense que je me débrouillerai quand même:* I don't have much money but I think I'll get along all the same.

dedans. *On l'a mis dedans:* they took him in, deceived him; they put him in jail.

dégueulasse: disgusting, filthy. *Je ne vous recommande pas de le fréquenter; c'est un type dégueulasse:* I don't advise you to associate with him; he's a disgusting fellow.

déjà. Notice the following slang uses:

C'est déjà pas si peu: that's not so little after all.

Quand est-ce qu'il va arriver déjà?: now let's see, when is he arriving?

demander. *Je vous demande un peu!:* who ever heard of such a thing! just imagine! I ask you! *Je vous demande un peu si c'est raisonnable!:* now I ask you, is that sensible?

diable. As an expletive, *diable!:* the deuce, the devil.

Que diable veux-tu faire?: what the deuce do you want to do?

C'est un grand diable: he's a big gawky fellow.

C'est un méchant diable: he is an evil fellow.

Il est assez bon diable: he is a rather good sort.

C'est un pauvre diable: he's a poor devil.

avoir le diable au corps: to be full of the devil

dire. Some popular slang uses:

(Il n')y a pas à dire: there's no denying it.

Je ne vous dis que ça: take my word for it; believe me!

C'est pas pour dire: I don't want to make an issue of it.

Ça ne me dit rien: that doesn't appeal to me; I don't like that.

Dites donc!: look here! I say!

doigt. "Finger," of course, but note the following interesting expressions:

Mon petit doigt me l'a dit: a little bird told me.

Il était à deux doigts de la mort: he was within an ace of death.

Vous avez mis le doigt dessus: you have hit the nail on the head; you've put your finger on it.

se fourrer le doigt dans l'oeil jusqu'au coude: to put one's foot in it, to deceive oneself most blindly

dos. Literally, "back." *En avoir plein le dos:* to be fed up (with someone or something). *J'en avais plein le dos de mon boulot:* I was fed up with my job.

drap. The word for "sheet" is used in the ironical expression *être dans de beaux draps:* to be in a pretty pickle, in a fine mess.

drôle: strange, curious, queer. *Il a une drôle de tête:* he has a queer face.

eau. *Etre en eau:* to be bathed in perspiration. *J'étais en eau après la partie de tennis:* I was drenched with perspiration after the tennis match.

s'emballer: to get excited, be carried away. *Tu t'emballes trop vite:* you are carried away too easily. *Ne vous emballez pas:* keep your shirt on.

embêter: to bother, disturb, bore. *Elle ne fait que m'embêter, je voudrais qu'elle parte:* she's only bothering me, I wish she'd leave.

s'embêter: to be bored, annoyed. *Je me suis embêté ter-*

riblement cette après-midi: I was terribly bored this afternoon.

embêtant: annoying. *C'est embêtant, ça:* it's a nuisance. *C'est embêtant de devoir sortir par ce temps:* it's annoying to have to go out in this weather.

embêtement: nuisance, bother

empoisonnant: very boring, rotten. *Un film empoisonnant:* a rotten picture.

encaisser: to be punished, receive blows. *Dans la vie, il faut apprendre à encaisser les coups avec grâce:* in life one must learn to suffer blows with grace.

engueuler: to abuse, scold. *Il est de mauvaise humeur parce qu'il s'est fait engueuler par son professeur:* he's in a bad mood because he was scolded by his teacher.

enragé. *Etre enragé pour:* to be keen on, wild about. *Je suis une enragée pour les sports d'hiver:* I'm keen on winter sports. *Ma soeur est une sportive enragée:* my sister is a tireless sportswoman.

envoyer. *Envoyer promener:* to send away, get rid of. *S'il vient vous embêter, envoyez-le se promener:* if he comes to bother you, get rid of him.

épatant. This word is used very much to show one's admiration and may be translated as "extraordinary, wonderful, terrific." *C'est épatant comme il nage:* it's really terrific, the way he swims.

épater: to astonish, show off, attract attention. *Si vous voulez épater vos amis ce soir, mettez donc votre robe en velours noir:* if you want to show off for your friends tonight, put on your black velvet dress.

éponge: sponge. *Passons l'éponge là-dessus:* let bygones be bygones.

espèce. Used for emphasis in insulting expletives, such as: *Espèce d'imbécile!:* you confounded fool!

estomac. *Avoir l'estomac dans les talons:* to be famished.

état. *Se mettre dans tous ses états:* to get very excited. *Pour un rien elle se met dans tous ses états:* she gets very excited over a mere trifle.

être. Some popular uses:

être très bien avec quelqu'un: to be on very good terms with someone

On y est très bien: the accomodations there are very good.

Je n'y suis pour rien: I have nothing to do with it.

Je n'y suis pour personne: I am not at home to anybody.

extra. Used as an adjective to indicate great pleasure or enjoyment. *Est-ce que la pièce vous a plu?—Oui, elle était extra:* did you like the play?—Yes, it was wonderful.

fainéant: lazy, idle. *Je vous préviens que je suis très fainéant et généralement fais la grasse matinée:* I warn you that I am very lazy and generally lie in bed late.

faire. Some popular uses:

Ça fait chic, jeune, vieux: it makes you look smart, young, old.

Faites donc: go right ahead, that's quite all right. (Example: A waiter is busy and apologizes to a customer for keeping him waiting. The customer might then use this expression.)

Cela ne me fait ni chaud ni froid: it doesn't matter to me one way or the other.

Cela ne me fait rien: it doesn't matter. *Cela ne me fait rien d'attendre:* I don't mind waiting.

Cela se fait maintenant: that is the fashion now.

Cela ne se fait pas: that is not the correct thing; it is not done; it is not proper.

faire des siennes: to be up to one's old tricks

se faire à: to get used to, accustom oneself to. *Le travail n'est pas très intéressant, mais je m'y ferai:* the work is not very interesting, but I'll get used to it.

ne pas s'en faire: not to worry. *Il ne faut pas s'en faire:* you must not worry about it. *Je ne m'en fais pas pour ça:* that doesn't bother me.

fauché: dead broke.

ficher. Often used in place of a more vulgar unprintable expression in a variety of uses.

Fiche-le ici: put it here.

ficher le camp: to beat it, scram. *Dépêchons-nous et fichons le camp:* let's hurry up and beat it.

ficher la paix: to shut up and stop bothering. *Fiche-moi la paix!:* shut up and leave me alone!

se ficher de: to laugh at, not give a damn. *Je m'en fiche!:* I don't give a damn!

se contreficher. Intensive form of *se ficher. Il se contrefiche de ce que ses beaux-parents pensent de lui:* he doesn't give a damn what his in-laws think of him.

fichu: shaped, done. *Elle est bien fichue:* she's well built; she's well dressed. *Sa robe est bien mal fichue:* her dress is quite a mess.

When applied to things, *fichu* may also mean "rotten, wretched." *Quel fichu temps!:* what rotten weather! With persons it may mean "likely, capable." *Elle est fichue d'oublier notre rendez-vous:* she's likely to forget about our appointment. *Je ne suis pas fichu de réparer la radio:* I'm not able to fix the radio.

filer: to be off, leave. *Il faut filer:* we must be off. *Filer à l'anglaise:* to take French leave

fille. Be careful with this word. It means "daughter," of course, but may also mean "prostitute, streetwalker, broad, girl, dame, etc." To be safe, use *jeune fille* for "girl, young lady."

foncer: to speed. *Il a foncé à toute vitesse dans la direction de Paris:* he went at full speed toward Paris.

fou. "Mad, crazy" in correct French, but notice its additional meanings in slang:

C'est fou: it's marvelous, astounding, amazing. *C'est fou ce qu'il y avait du monde à l'Opéra!:* it's astounding, the crowd there was at the Opera!

Le spectacle a eu un succès fou: the show had a tremendous success, was a great hit.

avoir un argent fou: to have lots of money. *Ça m'a coûté un argent fou:* that cost me a pile of money.

être fou à lier: to be raving mad

le fou rire: uncontrollable laughter. *J'avais le fou rire:* I just couldn't stop laughing.

fourcher. Literally "to fork, branch off." *La langue lui a fourché:* he made a slip of the tongue.

fourrer: to put. *Fourrez ça sur le divan:* put that on the sofa. *Mais où donc s'est-elle fourrée?:* but where did she hide herself?

frangin: brother; *frangine:* sister. *Mon frangin fait son service militaire et ma frangine suit des cours à l'université:* my brother is doing his military service and my sister is taking courses at the university.

fric: money, dough, cost. *Tous ces projets sont très beaux, mais il faudra aussi se procurer du fric:* all these plans are very nice, but we'll have to get some money.

gaffe: blunder. *Faire une gaffe:* to make a blunder, put your foot in it.

galette: money, dough.

gaga: senile, half-witted. *Ça fait déjà cinq ans qu'il est gaga:* he's been senile for the past five years.

garce: prostitute, hussy.

gazer: to speed, step on the gas. *La route est bonne ici; on peut gazer:* the road's good here; you can step on it. By extension, *ça gaze:* things are going well. *Ça va gazer:* it looks like trouble is brewing; we're in for it.

gober: to believe readily, swallow. *Vous verrez qu'il ne gobera pas ça:* you'll see that he won't swallow that.

gosse: child, kid. *Les gosses jouent à la balle dans la rue:* the kids are playing ball in the street.

　être beau (belle) gosse: to be nice-looking

grue: prostitute, tart.

gueule: mouth, jaw, face, mug. This is a very popular slang word and has a variety of uses:

fermer la gueule: to shut up, dry up

casser la gueule: to beat up

faire une sale gueule: to look worried, have a long face

avoir la gueule de bois: to feel out of sorts, have a hangover. *Si tu ne cesses pas de boire, tu auras une gueule de bois demain:* if you don't stop drinking you'll have some hangover tomorrow!

gueuler: to shout, protest.

guigne: bad luck. *Le pauvre garçon, il est poursuivi par la guigne!:* this poor guy, he's haunted by bad luck!

hein?: An expletive meaning "eh? what?" or sometimes used colloquially instead of *n'est-ce pas? Ça t'a plu, hein?:* you liked it, didn't you? *Hein, que c'est beau ce film:* this picture is beautiful, eh?

infect: rotten, awful. *Un temps infect:* awful weather.

intéressant. *Etre dans un état intéressant:* to be pregnant.

jambe. Literally "leg."

Ça te fera une belle jambe! (ironical): a lot of good that will do you! It won't do you any good!

Il a des fourmis dans les jambes: he has ants in the pants.

joli. "Pretty," but in slang it is used ironically to mean a "pretty mess." *C'est du joli!:* a fine state of affairs!

jour. *Au jour d'aujourd'hui:* nowadays.

jugeotte: common sense. *Pour son âge il a beaucoup de jugeotte:* he has a lot of common sense for his age.

là. *Ah, là, là! Oh, là, là!:* expletives meaning "oh, oh; oh, dear me!" *Oh, là, là, qu'il fait froid!:* oh, how cold it is!
langue: tongue. *Il a la langue bien pendue:* he has the gift of gab.

maboul. One of the many terms in French slang for "crazy, nuts."
magot: lot of money, pile of money.
maigre. The word for "thin" is used in the expression *fausse maigre* which is applied to those women who appear thin but are not really so. It is considered to be a compliment.
mal. Used in slang in the expression *n'être pas mal:* not to be bad-looking. *Elle n'est pas mal, la nouvelle dactylo:* the new typist isn't bad-looking.
malin: clever, cute, difficult. *C'est un petit malin:* he's a cute little fellow. *Ça n'est pas bien malin:* this is not very difficult.

Note also the expression *faire le malin:* to show off, to try to be smart.
marmelade. Means "marmalade, jam," of course, but note also its use in the expression *être dans la marmelade:* to be in the soup, to be in trouble.
marotte: fad, hobby. *Que voulez-vous, les bouquins c'est sa marotte:* what do you want, books are his hobby.

marrant: very funny. *Il nous a raconté une histoire marrante:* he told us a very funny story.

    se marrer: to have a good laugh. *Allons, venez avec nous, je vous promets qu'on va se marrer:* do come with us, I promise you we will have a good laugh.

marre. This slang word appears in the expression *en avoir marre:* to be fed up with. *J'en ai marre de ce travail:* I have had enough of this job.

mégot: cigar, cigarette butt.

messieurs-dames: ladies and gentlemen. Popular formula of greeting on arrival or departure, even if only one person is present. It may be used as a cue that the party should break up and is usually more effective when accompanied by a significant look at the clock.

mince. Also *mince alors!* Common expletive meaning "darn it!"

miteux, miteuse. This adjective derives from *mite* ("moth"), and in slang means "poor, shabby-looking." *Elle portait un ensemble miteux:* she was wearing a shabby-looking outfit.

moche: bad, of poor quality, ugly. *C'est moche comme moteur!:* it is a poor quality motor! *Elle n'est pas si moche que ça:* she is not as bad as all that.

môme: pretty girl, kid. *Je vais te présenter à la plus belle môme du quartier:* I am going to introduce you to the prettiest girl in the neighborhood.

se moquer. It means literally "to make fun of, to mock," but in slang it is used to render "not to care, not to give a darn."

Dites-lui que je m'en moque!: tell him that I don't give a darn! *Vous vous moquez du monde!*: you are joking, I presume!

mordre. *Ça ne mord pas*: it's no use trying, I won't fall for it.

nage. *Je suis en nage*: I am drenched with perspiration.

nerf. *Avoir les nerfs à fleur de peau*: to be extremely sensitive, to be jumpy.

nez. "Nose" of course, but in slang it is used in several interesting expressions:

mener par le bout du nez: to lead around by the nose. *Sa femme le mène par le bout du nez*: his wife leads him around by the nose.

Il fourre son nez partout: he butts in everywhere.

On lui a tiré les vers du nez: they pumped him.

J'en ai plein le nez: I am fed up.

noce. *Faire la noce*: to go on a spree (literally, to enjoy oneself as a guest at a wedding).

nom. *Nom de Dieu, nom d'un chien, nom d'une pipe*: expletives roughly equivalent to "good Lord, ye gods!"

nouvelles. *Vous m'en direz des nouvelles*: you will rave about it, you will be delighted with it. *Buvez ce café, vous m'en direz des nouvelles!*: drink this coffee, you'll rave about it.

nue. It is not used as much in correct French (where it means "high cloud") as it is in slang.

tomber des nues: to be amazed, to be astounded. *Je suis*

tombée des nues quand je l'ai vu avec la petite blonde: I was amazed to see him with that little blonde.

porter quelqu'un jusqu'aux nues: to laud, to praise

numéro: fellow, character, card. *As-tu jamais vu un tel numéro?:* did you ever see such a character?

oeil. This word is amply used in slang, as evidenced by the variety of expressions in which it appears:

mon oeil!: my eye! I should say not!

à l'oeil: free, without paying. *Il se débrouille toujours pour dîner à l'oeil:* he always manages to dine free.

coûter les yeux de la tête: to cost a small fortune

avoir les yeux au beurre noir: to have black eyes

Il ne le fera pas pour vos beaux yeux: he will not do it for you for nothing.

faire de l'oeil à quelqu'un: to make (amorous) eyes at someone

taper dans l'oeil de quelqu'un: to take someone's fancy

voir du même oeil que quelqu'un: to see eye to eye with someone

Cela saute aux yeux: that is as clear as can be.

fondre à vue d'oeil: to go down in weight rapidly, to melt away

avoir les yeux battus: to look tired around the eyes

oignon (pronounced *ognon*). It means, of course, "onion," but in slang, *c'est pas tes oignons* means "it's none of your business."

original. *C'est un original:* he is a queer duck; he is a strange fellow.

pagaille: disorder, confusion. *Le jour de mon départ, tout était en pagaille dans mon appartement:* the day of my departure, everything was in disorder in my apartment.

page. *Etre à la page:* to be up to date. *Ma grand-mère est très à la page:* my grandmother is very much up to date.

Panam. Affectionate slang term for Paris.

parler. Note the following slang uses:

Tu parles!: you said it! I should say so!

Vous parlez d'un examen!: it was some exam!

Voilà qui est parler, voilà qui s'appelle parler, or *c'est parler, cela:* now you are talking.

parler de la pluie et du beau temps: to talk about the weather; to talk of nothing in particular

pâte. *C'est une bonne pâte:* he (or she) is a good sort.

patte. Literally "paw," but in slang "hand, palm." *Il a dû graisser la patte à beaucoup de gens pour obtenir son poste:* he had to grease many people's palms to obtain his appointment. *A bas les pattes!:* keep your hands to yourself!

pavé. It is easily seen how this word which means "sidewalk" has come to render the idea of "to be out of work" in the slang expression *être sur le pavé.*

payer. Used in a variety of expressions:

Tu me le payeras!: I'll get even with you!

se payer la tête de quelqu'un: to pull someone's leg, kid someone. *Il veut se payer ma tête:* he wants to pull my leg.

C'est bien payé: it's more than enough!

peau. *Avoir quelqu'un dans la peau:* to be madly in love with someone. *Elle l'a quitté il y a longtemps, mais il l'a* *toujours dans la peau:* she left him a long time ago, but he's still madly in love with her.

Je ne voudrais pas être dans sa peau: I shouldn't like to be in his shoes.

pelotage: cuddling. *Pas de pelotage avant le mariage:* no lovemaking before marriage.

penser. *Pensez-vous! penses-tu!:* I should say not! you have another think coming! *Tu crois qu'il viendra en voiture? Penses-tu, par le temps qu'il fait!:* do you think he'll come by car? Not likely with this weather!

peu. *Ecoutez un peu:* just listen. *Regardez un peu:* just look. *Voyons un peu:* now let's see.

pic. *Arriver, tomber à pic:* to arrive in the nick of time, come in handy. *L'argent que ma tante m'a envoyé tombe vraiment à pic:* the money which my aunt sent me really came in the nick of time.

piger: to understand, to see, to look, to get, to catch. *Elle ne pige pas l'algèbre:* she can't understand algebra. *Pige-moi cette belle môme:* look at that pretty girl. *Il a pigé une grippe:* he caught the grippe.

pinard. Slang term for "wine."

plancher. *Débarrasse-moi le plancher:* get out of my way (literally, rid the floor of yourself).

plaquer: to chuck, to forsake someone, to abandon. *Sa femme l'a plaqué:* his wife left him.

plein. *J'en ai plein le dos de toutes ces complications:* I am fed up with all these complications.

pleurer. *Pleurer comme une Madeleine, pleurer comme un veau:* to cry like a baby, to cry abundantly.

poil. *A poil:* naked. *J'ai dû me mettre à poil pour la visite médicale:* I had to strip naked for the medical examination.

point. *Un point, c'est tout:* so much for that; and that's that.

poire. "Pear" literally, but in slang "dope, jerk, sucker." *C'est une vraie poire:* he's a real dope.

poisson. *Poisson d'avril:* April fool.

pomme. The word for "apple" is used in several slang expressions.

    ma pomme: myself. (*"Ma pomme, c'est moi"* is a line in a popular song.)

    tomber dans les pommes: to faint

    Note that *pommes de terre* (potatoes) is often shortened to *pommes. Pommes frites:* fried potatoes.

popote: cooking. *Faire la popote:* to cook the meals. *Ma femme est en train de faire la popote:* my wife is cooking (the meal).

pot. *On a découvert le pot aux roses:* they have discovered the mystery, the secret.

    tourner autour du pot: to beat about the bush

poudre. *N'avoir pas inventé la poudre:* not to be very bright.

    jeter de la poudre aux yeux: to throw dust in someone's eyes, to bluff someone

poule. In correct French it means, of course, "hen," but in slang it is used in the sense of "woman, broad, dame." *Je l'ai rencontré hier soir avec une belle poule:* I met him last night with a beautiful dame.

    poule mouillée: sissy, effeminate

princesse. *Aux frais de la princesse:* at the public expense. *Le dernier bal donné par le maire était aux frais de la princesse:* the last ball given by the mayor was at public expense.

purée. Literally, it means "thick soup, mash." In slang it is "distress, poverty." *Il est dans la purée:* he is flat broke.

putain: prostitute. Avoid using because it is quite vulgar.

quoi. Frequently used by many people to emphasize what has been said and may be variously translated as "do you see what I mean?, in short, don't you think so?" etc. *Voyez donc ce coucher de soleil; c'est beau, quoi?:* look at this sunset; it is beautiful, don't you think so? *Elle ne l'aime plus, quoi!:* in short, she no longer loves him. *C'est la guerre, quoi!:* it's war, what can you expect? *Je lui ai dit que j'étais fatiguée, quoi!:* I told him that I was tired, and that's all there was to it.

râclée: thrashing. *Votre fils mérite une bonne râclée:* your son deserves a good thrashing.

radis. In slang this word, which in correct French means "radish," appears in the expression *ne pas avoir un radis:* not to have a red cent. *Soyez gentil et emmenez-moi dîner, car je n'ai pas un radis:* be nice and take me out to dinner because I haven't got a red cent.

raide. *En raconter des raides:* to tell tall stories or smutty stories.

    Ça c'est un peu raide: that's a bit too much.

râler: to fume with anger. *Sa conduite m'a fait râler:* his behavior made me fume with anger.

raser. Although in correct French this is the word for "to shave," in slang it means "to bore." *Ne l'invitez pas car il va raser tout le monde:* don't invite him because he'll bore everybody.

    rasoir, raseur: a bore

rater: to miss, fail. *J'ai raté mon avion:* I missed my plane. *Il a raté son examen:* he failed his exam.

revenir. *Je n'en reviens pas:* I can't get over it. *Sa figure me revient:* I like his face.

rigoler: to laugh. *Tu me fais rigoler:* you make me laugh.

    rigolo: comical, funny. *Avez-vous jamais vu quoi que ce soit d'aussi rigolo?:* did you ever see anything that funny?

rire. *Vous voulez rire!:* you are joking, aren't you? you are not serious, are you?

rond. *N'avoir pas le rond:* not to have a red cent.

    rond-de-cuir: white collar worker, pen-pusher

rosse: nasty. *Ce qu'il est rosse, le nouveau professeur d'anglais!:* he's quite nasty, the new English teacher.

    être rosse avec quelqu'un: to be nasty to someone

roulant: screamingly funny. *C'était un film roulant:* it was a screamingly funny picture.

rouleau. *Etre au bout de son rouleau:* to be at one's wits end.

rouler. Literally "to roll," but is used in slang for "to cheat, to deceive, to take in." *Voilà la boutique où j'ai été roulé:* here is the shop where I was taken in.

rouler sa bosse: to knock about a lot. *Il a roulé sa bosse à travers le monde:* he's knocked about the whole world over.

se rouler: to rock with laughter

rouquin: red-head.

rouspétance: resistance, opposition. *Faire de la rouspétance:* to resist, grumble.

rouspéter: to resist, grumble. *Il a rouspété, mais à la fin il a cédé:* he grumbled, but he finally gave in.

rouspéteur: fighter, grumbler

sacré: blessed, confounded. As in English, often used ironically. *Toute la sacrée* (or *sainte*) *journée:* the whole blessed day.

saint. *Je ne sais à quel saint me vouer:* I don't know which way to turn.

Sainte nitouche is derived from *sainte n'y touche*, shortened from *une sainte qui n'y touche pas*, and means an "extreme prude." *Ne vous fiez pas à ses airs de sainte nitouche:* don't trust those prudish looks of hers.

faire la sainte nitouche: to play the innocent

salade. Literally "salad" and in slang "confusion, mess." *Quelle salade!:* what a mess!

salaud: dirty person, louse. When used as an adjective, it means "low, mean." *Je ne veux plus avoir à faire avec ce salaud-là:* I don't want anything more to do with that louse. *C'est salaud ce qu'il t'a fait:* what he did to you was low.

119

sale. The correct meaning of this word ("dirty") has been intensified in slang and has come to mean "bad, worthless, rotten."

un sale type: a bad egg, a good-for-nothing

une sale gueule: an ugly mug

un sale coup: a dirty trick, a rotten trick, a treacherous blow

salé. *Payer un prix salé* certainly does not mean "to pay a sale price" but just the opposite, "to pay an exorbitant price."

saligaud. A variant of *salaud* meaning "dirty fellow."

salopard: mean, vile person, louse.

saloperie: trash, junk, worthless stuff, dirty trick. *Vous n'auriez jamais dû payer autant pour une telle saloperie:* you should never have paid so much for such junk. *Jamais je ne lui pardonnerai la saloperie qu'il vient de me faire:* I'll never forgive him for the dirty trick he's just played on me.

sang. *Se faire du mauvais sang:* to worry. *Il se fait beaucoup de mauvais sang à cause de la maladie de son père:* he's very worried because of his father's illness.

bon sang!: expletive expressing impatience, wonder, etc. May be rendered by "Good Lord!, Heavens! goodness!" *Bon sang, mais quand est-ce que vous apprendrez à conduire?:* Heavens, but when will you learn how to drive?

se sauver. May be used in slang in the sense of "to leave, be off" without the idea of "to save oneself." *Ma mère m'attend, il faut que je me sauve:* my mother is waiting for me, I must be off.

savoir. *Ne vouloir rien savoir:* to be unwilling to do something. *Je lui ai expliqué comment le faire mais il n'en veut rien savoir:* I explained to him how to do it but he just won't listen (i.e., take advice).

tout ce que je sais: adverbial phrase meaning "at any rate." *Je ne me souviens pas si elle est blonde ou brune; tout ce que je sais, c'est qu'elle est très jolie:* I don't remember whether she's a blonde or a brunette; at any rate, she's very pretty.

pas que je sache: not to my knowledge

en savoir long: to know a lot about something

scie: nuisance, worry, bother. *Quelle scie de devoir aller dîner chez les Dupont!:* what a nuisance to have to go to the Duponts' for dinner!

sec. *Boire sec:* to drink straight. *Je voudrais du whiskey sec:* I would like a straight whiskey.

être à sec: to be broke

Note that *sec* is also an abbreviation for *seconde* in the slang expression *faire quelque chose en cinq sec:* to do something in a jiffy (literally, in five seconds).

sèche: cigarette. *Ce qu'il était difficile de se procurer des sèches pendant la guerre!:* it sure was difficult to obtain cigarettes during the war!

sentir. *Je ne peux pas le sentir:* I cannot bear the sight of him.

sou. *Il est sans le sou:* he is penniless.

gagner des sous: to make money. *Ce n'est pas toujours facile de gagner des sous:* it's not always easy to make money.

soûlard: drunkard.

  soûlardise: drunkenness
sujet. In slang, may be used in speaking of annoying children, flighty young men, and real scoundrels. *C'est un*
  mauvais sujet: he is a bad egg.

taper. *Taper une lettre:* to type a letter.

  taper quelqu'un: to touch, to borrow money from someone

  taper dans l'oeil à quelqu'un: to take someone's fancy

  taper sur les nerfs or *le système:* to get on someone's
  nerves

  Le vin me tape à la tête: wine goes to my head.

  tapé: mad, touched
tapisserie. *Faire tapisserie:* to be a wallflower.
tas. This word, which literally means "heap, pile," is used in
  the slang expression *un tas de* in the sense of "a lot of,
  heaps, lots (of things)." *Il m'a raconté un tas de men-*
  songes: he told me a pack of lies. *J'ai un tas de soucis:* I
  have a lot of worries.

temps. *Se donner du bon temps:* to have a good time.
tenir. Note the following useful expressions:

  Cela ne tient pas debout: that won't hold water.

  Tiens!: hello! look! see! *Tiens, te voilà!:* hello, there
  you are! *Tiens! Il fait noir dehors:* look! It is dark outside.
tête. *Tenir* or *faire tête à quelqu'un:* to stand up to someone.

  n'en faire qu'à sa tête: to do just as one pleases, take
  nobody's advice

  faire une tête: to pull a long face

timbré: crazy, cracked.

toc: fake, sham, imitation. *Elle adore les bijoux en toc:* she loves imitation jewelry.

toqué. One of the many French slang words for "crazy, touched." It is also used in slang in *se toquer de* (to fall in love with, fall for) and *toqué de quelqu'un* (madly in love with someone).

se tordre: to split one's sides (with laughter). *Je me tordais de rire:* my sides were splitting with laughter.

  tordant: very comical, a scream. *C'est un film tordant:* it's a screamingly funny picture.

toujours. Used ironically for emphasis. *Tu peux toujours essayer:* you can always try (but it won't do you any good).

toupet. In slang this word does not mean "toupee" but "impudence cheek, nerve." *Elle a parlé à son professeur avec beaucoup de toupet:* she spoke to her teacher very impudently.

trac: nervousness, jitters, stage fright. *J'ai toujours le trac avant un examen:* I always get the jitters before an exam.

truc. A very handy substitute for a word that one has forgotten. *Où a-t-il mis le truc qu'il devait laisser ici?:* where did he put that what-do-you-call-it he was supposed to leave here?

tuyau. Literally "pipe, tube," but in slang "tip (at horse-racing, etc.), hint." *J'ai reçu un tuyau sur ce cheval:* I've had a tip on this horse.

  avoir des tuyaux: to be in the know

type: character, fellow, guy. *C'est un bon type:* he is a nice fellow. *C'est un sale type:* he is a bad egg. *Quel type!:* what a guy!

vache. *Parler français comme une vache espagnole:* to speak French very badly.

veine. In slang this word, which literally means "vein," is used in the sense of "(good) luck." *On dit que qui a de la veine au jeu n'en a pas en amour:* they say whoever is lucky in gambling is unlucky in love.

un coup de veine: a lucky break

vélo. Abbreviation of *vélocipède* used in slang for "bike." *On voit beaucoup de vélos dans les rues de Paris:* one sees many bikes on the streets of Paris.

vendre. In slang the verb for "to sell" means "to give a person away, tell a secret, betray." *Je vais te raconter ce qui s'est passé mais j'espère que tu ne me vendras pas:* I'm going to tell you what happened but I hope that you'll not give me away.

venir. *Je vous vois venir:* I see what you're driving at.

ventre. *Tomber à plat ventre:* to fall flat on one's face.

savoir ce que quelqu'un a dans le ventre: to know what a person is worth or what a person thinks

vérité. *C'est une vérité de (M. de) la Palisse:* it is a self-evident truth, an obvious fact. *M. de la Palisse* was the subject of a popular old poem:

> *M. de la Palisse est mort,*
> *Mort de maladie;*

> *Un quart d'heure avant sa mort*
> *Il était encore en vie.*

Je lui ai dit ses quatre vérités: I told him where to get off.

vieux. *Mon vieux:* my dear friend, old boy.

voir. In addition to the literal meaning of "to see," *voir* has various slang uses:

Voyons voir: let us see; show it to me.

Montrez voir: just let me see.

Je ne peux pas le voir: I can't bear the sight of him.

Voyons (interjection): let us see; come now; come, come.

voui. Popular pronunciation of *oui.*

vouloir. *Que veux-tu?* or *Que voulez-vous?:* well, it couldn't be helped; what did you expect? what can we do about it? *J'ai fini par le lui donner, que voulez-vous?:* I ended up by giving it to him, there you are.

zéro. *C'est un zéro:* he is a nonentity.

zut. Also *zut alors!* Interjection expressing anger, surprise, admiration or disappointment. *Vous avez oublié le livre? Zut alors!:* you have forgotten the book? Darn it!

IV. BON VOYAGE

*Indispensable travel tips of a practical and
linguistic nature*

General

Travel light! There is a tendency to take along more
than is really necessary and you will suffer the inconvenience
of too much luggage and extra tips to porters. Two medium-
sized suitcases should be sufficient for a trip of three months.
Where possible take clothes that are easily laundered and
that require little or no ironing. Be sure to take along a light
raincoat and comfortable shoes. Take a supply of your
drugs or check with your physician about their availability
abroad. You may insure your baggage at very low cost.

For general information and regulations, travel folders
and maps, write to the French Government Tourist Office,
located in New York at 610 Fifth Avenue. Other offices are
in Chicago, San Francisco, Los Angeles, Montreal and
London. In Paris, the French National Tourist Office, 8 avenue de l'Opéra, and American Express Company, 11 rue
Scribe, are at your service.

Money and Tipping

It is safe and convenient to take travellers' checks, mostly
in small denominations. These checks may be cashed in
banks, certain agencies, and authorized hotels. A small fee
(a little over one per cent) is charged for exchanging money,
so don't think that you have been short changed. If you are

going to do some shopping, bear in mind that most stores give a discount if payment is made in America dollars or travellers' checks.

The official rate of exchange at the present time is 4.95 francs to the dollar. One franc is, therefore, less than 20 cents. To calculate rapidly the approximate American equivalent it may be simpler to divide the number of francs by five.

There are coins of 1, 2, 5, 10, 20, and 50 centimes, 1 and 5 francs, and paper bills of 5, 50, 100 and 500 francs.

A good number of your francs are going to disappear in the form of tips (*pourboires*). It is therefore worth knowing when tipping is not necessary. In most hotels, restaurants and barber shops there is a *taxe de service* (10 to 15 per cent) which takes the place of the tip. If in doubt, ask if the bill is *service compris*. Even here, however, a small additional tip may not be amiss if the service has been very good.

In France it is necessary to give a tip of 10 per cent of your admission ticket to the usher who shows you to your seat in a theater or movie house. You must also pay for your program if you want one, and give the seller a small tip. A tip of about 15 per cent is expected by a bartender, but half a franc will satisfy doormen and rest room attendants. And corresponding to usual practice, you tip taxi drivers (about 15 per cent), porters (about one franc per piece in railroad stations, but twice as much at piers), and anyone else who renders a special service. It's a good idea to carry a pocketful of small coins at all times.

Hotels and Homes

Hotels of every description abound in Paris and other major French tourist centers. Official lists, grouping hotels in categories and giving prices, are available at Government Tourist Offices. Acceptable hotels at modest prices (under 10 francs a day) may be found in good locations. A service charge of about 15 per cent is added to the bill and is supposed to relieve the guest of the tipping chore. In some resort regions there are additional local taxes which may come to another 10 per cent.

Rooms with bath (showers are rare) are not too abundant, and they are expensive. If you are watching your pocketbook, take a room without bath. It will have a washstand, and you can order a bath whenever you wish for a fee of about 1 or 2 francs. Here's an idea for those who prefer a shower. There are a number of large, clean swimming pools, both indoor and outdoor, equipped with showers, in Paris. If you have the time, why not go to the pool and have the pleasure of a swim and a shower at the same time? It costs about the same as the bath fee.

If you intend to stay in Paris for a long period (a month or more), it may be worth your while to investigate the *pensions*, which offer room and board at modest rates.

Certain peculiarities of French houses and homes require a word of explanation. Our first floor or ground floor is the *rez-de-chaussée*. Second floor (one flight up) is *premier étage*, third floor (two flights up) is *deuxième étage*, etc. There may also be an *entresol*, "mezzanine."

In apartment houses and more modest hotels, the elevators (which look like half-open cages) are intended to take passengers up rather than down. After stepping out of the elevator at your floor, close the elevator door and push the *renvoi* button to send it back to the main floor. Otherwise it may stay at that level.

If you return late (after about 11) you may find the outside door locked, and it will be necessary for you to ring for the *concierge* (superintendent-janitor) to let you in.

To cut down the electricity bill, some hotels and most apartment houses have a hall lighting system known as the *minuterie*. Hall lights are turned off at about 11 P. M. If you want light in the hall, you must press a button (find out where it is during the day) and the lights will go on for about three minutes. Then darkness again. Try to get to your room fast, or study in advance the location of the other buttons (usually at least one per floor), so that you may have light for another few minutes.

At most hotels you may leave your shoes outside your room at night, and in the morning when you rise, they will shine.

Some useful expressions:

ascenseur: elevator

avec bain, sans bain: with bath, without bath

une chambre à un lit, une chambre pour une personne or *une chambre pour moi seul:* a single room

une chambre à deux lits: a room with two beds

une chambre à double lit: a room with a double bed

la clef or *clé:* the key

le directeur or *gérant:* the manager

la note: the bill
la serviette: the towel

Eating and Drinking

As with hotels, there are restaurants in Paris for every budget. An average meal at one of the many fancy restaurants may cost as much as 70 francs. For the less affluent tourist, however, there are numerous good places where a complete meal may be had for as little as six francs. Look around. Menus are posted in the windows of most restaurants. NOTE: Many of the inexpensive restaurants charge for bread, butter and napkins.

A typical French breakfast (*petit déjeuner*) consists of coffee or hot chocolate, a bun or sweet roll (*croissant, brioche*), and butter This breakfast is called *café complet.*

For lunch and dinner, the usual beverages are inexpensive red wine (*vin ordinaire*), beer (*bière*), carbonated or mineral water (*eau minérale*). All of these beverages are quite cheap. If you want water, ask for *une carafe d'eau.*

Cheeses (*fromages*), yogurt (*yaourt*) and fruits are regularly included among desserts.

In most restaurants the tip (10 to 15 per cent) is included in the bill and is listed on it as *service.* You may, however, leave some additional change if you wish. It is advisable to check the itemized bill and to count your change. Mistakes are sometimes made.

Useful restaurant vocabulary:
addition: check, bill. *L'addition, s'il vous plaît* or *ça fait*

combien, mademoiselle?: the check, please.

bistro. A popular term for a small restaurant or café

brasserie. A sort of tavern-restaurant

café. A delightful feature of Paris are the numerous sidewalk cafés where you may sit and relax and watch the crowds go by. You may order drinks (soft or hard) and light food.

café au lait or *café crême:* coffee with milk or cream

café nature or *café noir:* black coffee. The term *demi-tasse* is no longer current in French.

un couvert: a setting

crèmerie. A dairy-type restaurant

casse-croûte: light snacks, short orders

cure-dents: toothpick

garçon: waiter

mademoiselle: waitress

le plat du jour: the daily special

à la provençale: Provençal style, which means prepared with lots of garlic

thé complet: tea with choice of sandwiches and pastry

thé dansant. Afternoon tea and dancing, usually from four to six, at certain hotels and large cafés.

Shopping

You will no doubt do some shopping in Paris. The following pointers may be helpful.

Stores are generally closed on Sunday and Monday. Some, however, are open on Monday afternoons. The usual hours are 9 to 6:30, but except for some department stores, most shops shut down from 12 to 2 for lunch. It is an interesting experience to visit one of the large department stores *(les grands magasins)*. Most stores give a discount if payment is made in American dollars or travellers' checks. There is usually a sign to that effect in the window.

French clothing sizes, with the exception of gloves, do not correspond to their American equivalents. Here are some of the most popular American sizes followed by the French measurements in italics.

WOMEN'S DRESSES: Size 8—*38*; 10—*40*; 12—*42*; 14—*44*; 16—*46*; 18—*48*; 20—*50*. WOMEN'S SHOES: Size 5 to 5½—*36*; 6—*37*; 7—*38*; 7½—*39*; 8—*40*; 9—*41*; 10—*42*. WOMEN'S HATS: Size 21½—*55*; 22—*56*; 22½—*57*; 23—*58*; 23¼—*59*; 23½—*60*.

MEN'S SHIRTS: Size 13½—*34*; 14—*35* to *36*; 14½—*37*; 15—*38*; 16—*40* to *41*; 16½—*42*; 17—*43*. MEN'S SHOES: Size 5 to 5½—*37*; 6—*38*; 6½—*39*; 7 to 7½—*40*; 8—*41*; 8½—*42*; 9 to 9½—*43*; 10 to 10½—*44*; 11 to 11½—*45*; 12 to 12½—*46*. MEN'S HATS: Size 6⅞—*55*; 7—*56*; 7⅛—*57*; 7¼—*58*; 7⅜—*59*; 7½—*60*.

To ask the price:
Quel est le prix (de cet article)?
Le prix est de combien?
C'est combien?
Combien prenez-vous pour . . . ?
Combien est-ce què ça coûte?
(A good reply may be *Oh, c'est trop cher:* it's too dear.)

Faites-moi un prix raisonnable: Make me a reasonable price.

Quel est votre dernier prix?: What is your final (lowest) price?

Je désire acheter une robe dans les 200 francs: I should like to buy a dress for about 200 francs.

Additional vocabulary:

arrhes: deposit

la caisse: the cashier's desk

essayer: to try on

mademoiselle: Used to address a saleslady.

Monsieur (Madame) désire?: Can I help you? What can I do for you? The customer is often politely addressed in the third person.

la pointure: the size (of shoes, gloves, etc.)

soldes or *vente d'occasions:* sale, bargains

Travelling

One of the most interesting ways to see Paris is to wander about on foot. (Bring comfortable shoes!) A word of caution before you set out. Traffic is heavy and can be fatal to the absent-minded pedestrian. If possible, cross streets only in the nailed lanes (*passages cloutés*) reserved for pedestrians. A favorite monument, the *Arc de Triomphe,* underneath which is the Tomb of the Unknown Soldier, is located in the middle of the *Place de l'Etoile,* where traffic is especially bad. Be extremely careful here, or the Unknown Soldier you are attempting to visit may be joined by an Unknown Pedestrian.

Another inexpensive way of taking a tour of Paris is by

133

bus (*autobus*). Many bus routes cover the city, and if you avoid the rush hours they are quite comfortable. Near the bus stop there is a lamp post with a box containing numbered *tickets d'appel*. Take one as soon as you arrive. If the bus should be almost full, the conductor allows the passengers to board according to the numbers on these slips. Standing on buses is not permitted, except on the rear platform. If the bus is full, it will have a sign *complet,* or the conductor may say *complet.*

It is advisable to buy a booklet (*carnet*) containing twenty tickets. You will save about $\frac{1}{3}$ of the cost of individual tickets. After you have taken your seat, tell the conductor your destination and he will detach the required number of tickets, depending on the distance you travel. Bear in mind that most lines stop running at about midnight.

The subway (*Métro*) provides Paris with what is probably the most complete undercoverage of any city in the world, and will take you almost any place. As with buses, it is much more economical to buy a *carnet* of ten tickets each good for one fare.

Each train consists of a first class (red colored car marked I) and second class. The first class has leather-cushioned seats and is usually not crowded. Second class has wooden seats and is about $\frac{1}{3}$ cheaper than first class. If you ride first class a conductor or inspector (*contrôleur*) will probably come by to check your ticket.

It is important to remember that the train doors do not open automatically. If you want to enter or leave the train, after it stops unlock the latch and open the doors. The doors are closed (with a bang!) by automatic control. You will also come across the following safety device in Paris subways. As a train pulls into the station, an iron gate shuts, either automatically or controlled by a guard, preventing those who are not yet on the platform from rushing onto it and into the train. The gate is opened as the train leaves the station.

Large maps are posted at all subway entrances. At major stations, such as the Opéra, you may press a button for the station you want, and the map will light up in different colors showing the route and transfer points. A *métro* line is identified by the name of the last stop (*direction*). There are also maps inside the train showing its route and where it connects with other lines. When you leave the train, go to the exit marked *Correspondance* if you wish to transfer. The street exit is *Sortie*.

NOTE: Subway trains stop running at about 1 A. M.

More expensive than subway or bus, but hardly prohibitive, are the taxis. The fare is indicated on a meter, and the usual tip is 15 per cent. By day taxis are almost a bargain. After 11 P. M., however, the *tarif de nuit* is in effect, and the meter goes twice as fast. The cab driver is called *chauffeur*.

For long-distance travelling, Paris has several large railroad stations (*gares*). The Gare St. Lazare is best known to tourists because the boat trains use it. There is an English-speaking service in the main waiting room, although readers of this little book should not need it.

It may be advisable to consult American Express about getting train tickets, which is often a fairly complicated process even for the French. American Express will be able to give you up-to-date information and arrange for round-trip or other discounts.

There are two classes on French trains. First class: plush seats, six passengers to a compartment, and fairly expensive. Second class is quite comfortable, though the seats are less soft than in first class, eight passengers to a compartment, and about ⅔ the price of first class. For the average adventuresome young man or woman, we recommend second class as adequate, relatively inexpensive and interesting. If you must take a sleeper (available in first and in some second class trains), the *wagon-lit* ticket will just about double your fare. A *couchette* is a somewhat less expensive sleeper. Remember, however, that Paris is only about twelve hours from the most distant points in France.

There are round trip discounts on long distance trips as well as family tickets that can save you money.

Long-distance trains have a diner (*wagon-restaurant*) for which the conductor sometimes issues tickets. You may also purchase food at stations along the way.

There are four main types of French trains:

train de luxe: first class only; extra fare. Also the *auto-rails:* fast first class coach, only on certain runs; extra fare.

rapide: express train (a small extra fare)

express: not as fast as the *rapide*

omnibus: local train

NOTE: Don't throw away your ticket; it will be collected when you arrive at your destination.

Buses (*autocars*) travelling along scenic routes afford an opportunity to see more of the country. On long trips, buses stop for the night, and you sleep in a convenient hotel. The fare is about the same as second class by train.

If time is valuable and money isn't, you can fly to almost any part of France in less than two hours.

NOTE: Transportation systems almost always use the 24-hour timetable, explained below, page 139.

Useful travelling vocabulary:

un arrêt: a stop. *Arrêt facultatif:* stop on request (bus will stop if you signal). *Arrêt obligatoire:* compulsory stop.

un billet d'aller et retour: a round trip ticket; *une seconde pour Paris, simple* (or *aller seulement*): a one-way ticket to Paris, second class.

la banlieue: the suburbs

le buffet: the refreshment room

la consigne: the checkroom for baggage

de l'autre côte: on the other side

le couloir: the corridor

fumeurs, non-fumeurs: smokers, non-smokers

le guichet: the ticket window

un horaire or *indicateur:* a timetable

un oreiller: a pillow

ne pas se pencher en dehors: do not lean out (of the window)

porteur: porter

le quai: the platform

les renseignements: information

la salle d'attente: the waiting room

sens unique: one-way

un supplément: an extra fare

137

tout droit: straight ahead
valable: valid
la voie: the track
la voiture: the car. *En voiture!:* all aboard!

Measurements

The metric system is used in France for measuring distance, weight and capacity. A few figures should be a sufficient guide for most tourist needs.

A meter (*mètre*) is slightly more than 39 inches or 3¼ feet.

A *centimètre* (1/100 of a *mètre*) is about 4/10 of an inch.

A *kilomètre* (1000 *mètres*) is ⅝ of a mile.

100 *kilomètres* is approximately 62 miles.

A *kilogramme* (almost always called *kilo*) is 2.2 pounds.

½ *kilo* (500 *grammes*) is a little more than one pound.

10 *kilos* is 22 pounds.

50 *kilos* is 110 pounds.

75 *kilos* is 165 pounds.

A liter (*litre*) is slightly over one quart.

½ *litre* is approximately one pint.

4 *litres* is a little more than one gallon.

A *bidon* (can for gasoline) holds 5 *litres*.

In the Centigrade thermometer, 0° equals 32° Fahrenheit, 100° C = 212° F.

To convert Centigrade to Fahrenheit, multiply by 9/5 and add 32.

10° C = 50° F	25° C = 77° F
20° C = 68° F	30° C = 86° F

For non-mathematicians a rough guide for getting the approximate Fahrenheit temperature is to double the Centigrade and add 30. The result will generally be a few degrees above the correct Fahrenheit equivalent.

Railroads and other transportation systems use the 24-hour timetable, obviating the need of A.M. or P.M. From 1 A.M. to 12:59 in the afternoon the hour is self-explanatory; but 1 P.M. is 13 *heures*.

3 P.M. is 15 h.	12 midnight is 24 h.
8:30 P.M. is 20.30 h.	12:45 A.M. is 0.45 h.

Just subtract 12 to figure out the time.

Note that the 24-hour system is also used for theaters, meetings and other public functions.

Telephones

House and hotel phones require no special explanation. Just dial the number (example: OPEra 43-21). If you call from a pay station (in subways, railroad stations, post offices, cafés, etc.) you must use a slug *(jeton)* which you buy for about 50 centimes from the person in charge. (Some restaurants do not have pay phones, but add the charge to your bill.) Insert the *jeton* in the slot and dial the number. When someone answers, push the button near the hook for a moment to enable the person on the other end to hear you. You are then in normal telephonic communication.

In order to make a call to the suburbs of Paris (*banlieue*) ask for *Régional*; for a long distance call, ask for *Inter*.

A special convenience of the Paris telephone system is the SVP service. Just dial the letters SVP and you can ask for almost any kind of information—theater, shopping, social, etc.

Some telephone vocabulary:

allô: hello

un annuaire: a telephone directory

à l'appareil: on the phone, speaking. *Qui est à l'appareil?:* who's calling, please?

Il est au bout du fil: he's on the wire.

Ne coupez pas: don't hang up.

décrocher: to take off (the receiver)

J'écoute: speaking.

Ici Monsieur Berry: Mr. Berry speaking.

Une ligne, s'il vous plaît, mademoiselle: an outside wire, please, operator. (To hotel operator.) *La ligne est détraquée:* the line is out of order.

Le numéro n'est pas libre (or *est occupé*): the line is busy. *Mauvais numéro:* wrong number.

Ne quittez pas: hold the wire.

raccrocher: to hang up (the receiver)

Letters

If you do not have a definite address in Paris, have your mail sent c/o American Express, 11 rue Scribe, Paris 9ᵉ. You can pick it up when you arrive, and if your hotel is not far from American Express, you may want to continue using it as your mailing address. You may also leave written messages for friends in the mail room. No fee.

Letters to Paris should include the *arrondissement* number if known:

Mlle Geneviève François
87, rue de Seine
Paris 6ᵉ, France

Outside of Paris, you may have your mail sent c/o *Poste Restante* (General Delivery) for a nominal fee. If possible, include the *département*.

M. Gabriel Lovett
Poste Restante
Juan-les-Pins (Alpes Maritimes)
France

A letter to a hotel should be addressed:

Monsieur le Directeur
Hôtel Continental
Rouen (Seine-Inférieure)
France

Stamps (*timbres*) may be bought at post offices, tobacco stands, American Express, and most hotels.

To contact someone quickly by mail, try the *pneumatique* service. Use the special blue form and mail it in the proper box at the post office. Your special delivery letter (called *pneu* or *petit bleu*) is shot through tubes to the proper *arrondissement* and then delivered to the addressee. It costs between 1.25 and 2 francs and takes about two hours. It is a great convenience for reaching someone without a phone.

Abbreviations

arr. *arrivée*

av, Av. *Avenue*

bd, Bd., bld, Bld. *Boulevard*

Cie. *Compagnie*

dep. *départ*

fr. *franc*

h. *heure*

M. *Monsieur.*   MM. *Messieurs*

Mlle (not followed by period) *Mademoiselle*

Mme (not followed by period) *Madame*

P.T.T. *Postes, télégraphes, téléphones*

r. *rue*

R. de C. *rez-de-chaussée*

R. D. *Route Départementale*

R. N. *Route Nationale*

R.S.V.P. *Réponse, s'il vous plaît*

S. A. *Société Anonyme* ("Ltd.," or "Inc.")

S.N.C.F. *Société Nationale des Chemins de Fer Français* (The French National Railway System)

S.V.P. *S'il vous plaît*

T.S.F. *Télégraphie sans fil* ("radio")

V.O. *Version originale* (Movies spoken in their original language and not dubbed in French)

W.C. *Water Closet*

French Courtesy

Good manners are universal, but each country and language has certain special niceties which should be observed.

When speaking to a person, *monsieur, madame,* or *mademoiselle* must be used in almost every sentence. *Oui, monsieur; bonjour, madame* sound much better than a flat *oui* or *bonjour.* If in doubt about using *madame* or *mademoiselle,* by all means say *madame.* Tip your hat to men as well as to women, and shake hands on greeting and leaving. Use "please," "thank you," "you are welcome," and "pardon" even more than in English. Here are the best translations:

S'il vous plaît, je vous prie, voulez-vous bien (+ infinitive), *veuillez* (+ infinitive) all mean "please."

Merci bien is the usual way of saying "thank you." Also *merci beaucoup* and *merci mille fois.* Remember that *merci* alone may mean "no, thank you" when you are offered something.

The formal ways of saying "you're welcome" are *je vous en prie, à votre service* and *il n'y a pas de quoi.* Less formal and more common are *de rien* and *pas de quoi.*

Pardon, pardonnez-moi and *excusez-moi* are "pardon me, forgive me." *Plaît-il* (also *pardon*) is "I beg (your) pardon" when you don't hear something. When requesting information from a stranger, always begin with *pardon, monsieur (madame, mademoiselle).*

For greeting acquaintances, *Comment allez-vous?* is rather stiff. Much more usual is *(Comment) ça va?* Among close friends, *salut* is often heard.

On being introduced, the usual acknowledgment is *enchanté* or *charmé.* For formal occasions it may be preferable to use a whole sentence:

—*Enchanté de faire votre connaissance, monsieur.*

143

—*Tout le plaisir est pour moi, monsieur.*

These forms may be varied by merely nodding and saying *monsieur, madame* or *mademoiselle*.

—*Permettez-moi de vous présenter Madame Dubois.*

—*Madame.*

Variants for *au revoir* are *au plaisir* (rather formal), *à tout à l'heure* and *à bientôt* (both meaning "see you soon"), and *salut* (among close friends).

To win French friends and make a favorable impression, it is very important to try to speak the language. They will appreciate this gesture of friendship and interest, and will help make your trip more meaningful and enjoyable.

Bon voyage et bonne chance!